What Are They Saying About the Trinity?

Anne Hunt

PAULIST PRESS
New York/Mahwah, N.J.

Cover design by James F. Brisson

Library of Congress Cataloging-in-Publication Data

Hunt, Anne, 1952–
    What are they saying about the Trinity? / Anne Hunt.
        p.   cm.
    Includes bibliographical references.
    ISBN 0–8091–3806–9 (alk. paper)
    1. Trinity—History of doctrines—20th century. 2. Catholic Church—Doctrines—History—20th century. I. Title.
BT109.H86   1998
231′.044—dc21   98–18074
                                                                                        CIP

Published by Paulist Press
997 Macarthur Boulevard
Mahwah, New Jersey 07430

Printed and bound in the
United States of America

Contents

1. Introduction 1

2. The Trinity and Latin American Liberation Theology 8

3. The Trinity and Christian Feminist
   Liberation Theologies 22

4. Ecological Approaches to the Trinity 35

5. The Trinity and Jesus' Paschal Mystery—
   Hans Urs von Balthasar 49

6. Trinity of Love: The Psychological
   Analogy Revisted 62

7. Conclusion 75

Notes 84

Selected Bibliography and Recommended Reading 93

To My Sister Jill, with Love.

1
Introduction

Even a very brief survey of contemporary trinitarian theology shows that theologians, from a variety of perspectives, are showing striking creativity and imagination in their efforts to render the mystery which lies at the very heart of our Christian faith meaningful and effective for the transformation of culture and society. In this small book, I will be attempting to sketch five typical developments in contemporary trinitarian theology. My purpose, apart from giving a brief objective outline of the theologies treated, is to communicate something of the excitement evident in such explorations.

Classical trinitarian theology developed with the great trinitarian controversies and the ecumenical councils of the fourth century. The Arian controversy prompted a clear response to the question of the divinity of Jesus Christ. The Council of Nicaea (325) in fact gave a radical answer. Employing the nonbiblical term *homoousios* (of the same substance), the Council defined that the Son was indeed truly God. Since then, Christians from East to West have proclaimed, in the words of the Creed, that the Son is "of one being with the Father, God from God, light from light, true God from true God."[1] The proclamation of *homoousios,* the consubstantiality of the Son and Father, by the Council of Nicaea in 325, and later that of the coequal divinity of the Holy Spirit by the Council of Constantinople in 381, settled the problem as to what constituted orthodox trinitarian doctrine. But the perennial theological challenge then, as in every age, remained as to how to understand the trinitarian faith we confess, and how to speak in ways that are disclosive and persuasive of its essential meaning.

A century after the great ecumenical Council of Nicaea, Augustine of Hippo laid the foundation for what became the classical approach to an explication of this great mystery in the Latin theological tradition.[2] In his treatment of the mystery, he gives consideration first to the divine unity. He then proceeds to a reflection on the Trinity, considering first the missions, then the relationships between the Three, and finally he treats the immanent processions within the godhead. Basing himself on the biblical understanding of the human person as created in the image of God (Gn 1:26–27), Augustine explores a number of triads drawn from reflection on the human person as self-conscious subject as a means to understand the processions of the Son and Spirit.[3] Through these analogies, each a version of what is now commonly termed "the psychological analogy," the processions are tentatively explained chiefly in terms of our conscious experience of knowing and loving God. By analogy, God is fully conscious and knows and loves God-self and creation. Such analogical thinking clearly had its own plausibility and persuasiveness, grounded as securely as it was in fundamental human and Christian experience.

Almost a millennium later, the great medieval theologian Thomas Aquinas transposed the psychological analogy from its deeply and recognizably experiential roots in Augustine's theology, to the more refined technical terminology and framework afforded by Aristotelian philosophy.[4] In contrast to Augustine's more immediately historical approach, Aquinas's treatment of the mystery of the Trinity progresses from the processions and the relationships of the divine persons *ad intra,* and then to the divine missions *ad extra.* Aquinas's concern in writing his *Summa Theologiae,* which he intended as a textbook for beginners,[5] is systematic intelligibility and explication of the mystery; hence he employs a different method and approach compared to Augustine. The resultant synthesis is an unsurpassed achievement in logical coherence, scientific precision, and systematic rigor—an elegant and sophisticated exercise in analogical thinking. It is no wonder that the Thomistic synthesis of the mystery of the Trinity constituted the classical form and *ordo doctrinae* of trinitarian teaching through the centuries, right down to our era.

But, in the mid-twentieth century, serious questions have surfaced as to the usefulness and meaningfulness of the traditional form of Latin trinitarian theology. Elegant and sophisticated though it is, the Thomistic synthesis is found wanting, criticized for being remote from biblical witness and the events of salvation history wherein the mystery of the Trinity was revealed, remote from our experience, and so utterly abstract as to be practically meaningless. Even Karl Rahner commented that the psychological theory of the Trinity has "the disadvantage that in the doctrine of the Trinity it does not really give enough weight to a starting point in the history of revelation and dogma which is within the *historical and salvific* experience of the Son and of the Spirit as the reality of the divine self-communication to us, so that we can understand from this historical experience what the doctrine of the divine Trinity really means."[6] Although the psychological analogy takes seriously the biblical assertion that the human person is created in the image of God, it is criticized as not taking seriously enough the actual events in the economy of salvation history. Whatever the reasons for it, an understanding of and devotion to the Trinity does seem demonstrably remote from the faith-life of most members of the Christian community. While criticisms leveled again Augustinian-Thomistic trinitarian theology are not always well directed or well informed, that mode of explication of the mystery is clearly no longer readily effective in the contemporary context, both in our modern search for self and in our culture's search for God in the midst of our struggle against the enormous power of evil that so manifestly besets us.

Meanwhile, in contemporary academic theological circles, controversy over the relationship between the immanent and economic Trinities (as distinct from previous considerations in terms of God *ad extra* and *ad intra*) has been keen. Karl Rahner threw this issue into prominence with his contentious *Grundaxiom* that the economic Trinity is the immanent Trinity and vice versa.[7] Yet really, the very statement of Rahner's *Grundaxiom* was itself indicative of the separation that had developed between economic and immanent considerations in trinitarian theology and of the more general remoteness of trinitarian theology from day-to-day Christian life and from the mainstream of theological issues and concerns.

Yet, the Trinity is utterly central and fundamental to our faith as Christians. Both the formula of baptism and the Nicene Creed attest to it, as well as the structure of the liturgy of the eucharist which we celebrate. In the daily round of Christian liturgy and devotion, we begin and end our prayers with the sign of the cross and the formula, "In the name of the Father and of the Son and of the Holy Spirit," and offer the trinitarian doxology, "Glory be to the Father and of the Son and of the Holy Spirit, as it was in the beginning is now and ever shall be, world without end." The Trinity is a sacred symbol of vital importance to our contemporary world and church. Whatever our experience of the Trinity, whatever our actual understanding of this great mystery, trinitarian rhetoric abounds and trinitarian meaning is obviously there to be found.

How, then, might theology serve faith in the recovery of its trinitarian significance? If our credal affirmations of the mystery of the Trinity are true, then they must be very true, affecting profoundly every dimension of our existence. Such a question and such a presumption serve to plot the direction of the exposition that is to follow. Given the excitement and exuberance of current trinitarian theologies, we must, however, confine ourselves to a certain scope. Hence, despite the interfaith and ecumenical range of trinitarian interest and concern, I propose to limit this study to recent developments in Roman Catholic theology, leaving the broader survey to more comprehensive scholarly studies. I hope that the five new ways of imagining the Trinity explored here will serve as a useful introduction to the direction trinitarian theology is currently taking.

A word, then, on each of the approaches I intend to sketch:

1. Latin American liberation theology seeks to reclaim trinitarian theology for its specific purposes and its own particular perspective: that of the poor and their liberation. The energies of liberation theology are nourished by the recognition of the three divine persons as a communion of coequals that is characterized by relationality and mutuality. From this perspective, the Trinity can be understood as a prototype of human society motivating social and historical progress. Through the revelation of the Trinity, society is summoned to transform itself after the model of the trinitarian communion. In this regard, we shall consider the work of Brazilian theologian Leonardo Boff.

2. Christian feminist theology, arising from women's experience of exclusion and oppression in society generally and in the church in particular, looks for a more radical critical feminist retrieval of the trinitarian symbol. Those intent on the liberation of women have come to recognize that the classical explication of the Trinity has, to some degree, been affected by sexism. In the work of North American theologian Elizabeth Johnson, who seeks to reclaim the biblical image of God as Sophia using expressly female imagery for *each* of the three divine persons, we find a remarkable and thought-provoking reconstruction of trinitarian theology that is acutely attune to these issues.

3. An interconnection between ecological and trinitarian concerns, prompted by the current ecological crises and an emerging ecological consciousness in our culture, is found in the work of Australian theologian Denis Edwards. He finds rich resources in Wisdom Christology, together with the comparatively neglected trinitarian theologies of the medieval

theologians Richard of St. Victor and Bonaventure, to construct an intentionally ecological theology that is firmly based
on a systematic understanding of the trinitarian God.

4. The trinitarian theology of the Swiss theologian Hans Urs
von Balthasar is the fruit of his aesthetically-charged contem-
plation of the relationship of the Trinity to the paschal mystery of Jesus' death and resurrection. It was, after all, through
the disciples' experience of the three holy days—the *Sacrum
Triduum*—that they were led to proclaim that Jesus is Lord
and that God is these Three. Von Balthasar rejects the classical psychological analogy and seeks to return to the biblical
witness. What is particularly striking about his trinitarian theology is the emphasis he gives to Jesus' descent into hell. In
this way, von Balthasar forges a trinitarian theology of
remarkable power and inspiration which resonates with modern Christian experience and strikes deep chords with the
contemporary affective experience of the self.

5. Since each of these four authors, some more determinedly than
others, effectively sets aside the classical Augustinian-
Thomistic synthesis of the mystery of the Trinity and the psychological analogy, we are left with an urgent and important
question: Is the psychological analogy hopelessly beyond
retrieval? It has, however, served to explicate the mystery of the
three-person of God for centuries and surely cannot be hastily
dismissed. It is grounded in the ancient biblical assertion that
the human person is created in the image of God (Gn 1:26–27).
It is justified biblically in the New Testament revelation of God
as Word and Love, which surely pertains to the divine consciousness. Might it be the now-outmoded metaphysical wrappings of the classical form of trinitarian theology that make it
unpalatable to us now, but which perhaps in fact conceals a
profound trinitarian truth that is there to be retrieved? Here we
turn to Australian Redemptorist theologian Tony Kelly who,

following the more traditionally systematic approach to the mystery of the Trinity, aims to promote a critical retrieval of the classical tradition of trinitarian theology. By transposing the psychological analogy into the terms of Bernard Lonergan's intentionality analysis of the conscious, intending human subject, wherein the peak state of consciousness is being-in-love, Kelly makes a correlation between human being-in-love and the foundational Christian experience of God as Love, as Being-in-Love. In this way, he recasts the Thomistic trinitarian theology wherein God is Be-ing, pure being, in terms of God as Being-in-Love, and from thence proceeds to tease out the meaning of the Trinity in its contemporary cosmic, ecological, psychological, political, and interfaith dimensions. The psychological analogy, thus transposed, emerges with new concreteness and considerable fruitfulness.

We shall look at the salient themes and essential characteristics of the trinitarian theology which emerges in each of these new imaginings. My aim throughout is to introduce the reader to these new areas of trinitarian imagination, to offer a helpful overview of the development and to whet the theological appetite for further reading and reflection. My ultimate aim is that of the authors whose work we will now begin to explore: that all of us grow into a more conscious, more loving, and more faithful relationship with the radiant and life-giving mystery of our triune God.

Even though this account is already limited to five typical approaches in the Roman Catholic theological tradition, there will still be particular traditional questions that cannot be directly addressed, such as the "filioque controversy" concerning the procession of the Holy Spirit. These, together with many ecumenical and interfaith considerations, must be deferred to a fuller treatment at a later time.[8] So within the stated limitations, let us proceed to sample something of the extraordinary creativity that is evident in the Catholic tradition in the field of trinitarian theology.

2
The Trinity and Latin American Liberation Theology

Vatican II, in its Pastoral Constitution on the Church in the Modern World, *Gaudium et Spes,* made its own "the joys and the hopes, the griefs and the anxieties" of all humanity, but "especially those who are poor or in any way afflicted." It beckoned the church to read "the signs of the times" in order more effectively to be the sacrament of salvation to the world. Emphasizing an understanding of church as the people of God engaged in the historical process constituting "the modern world," Vatican Council II called for critical reflection on people's lived reality in the light of faith and its contemporary experience of society and culture. Since such reflection on experience has inescapable particularities in vastly differing contexts throughout the world, the way was opened for local churches to take their own respective situations as the starting point for theological reflection and evangelization. A new surge of theological creativity ensued.

The Council's openness and wealth of theological insight gave a singular impetus to the church in Latin America, whose contribution to theological development until the time of Vatican II and even at the Council had been minimal. Prompted by Vatican II, Latin American theologians returned to the scriptures and to the Christian theological tradition with very new eyes, for critical reflection in the light of faith on the lived reality of people in

Latin America compels one to attend to the experience of appalling oppression of the masses of the poor. It is therefore the poor who occupy the central position in the reflections of what has come to be known as "Latin American liberation theology." In this way, the situation of the oppressed became a new *locus theologicus*—the agonizing point of departure from which to restructure both the concerns and the methods of theology.[9]

Gustavo Gutiérrez's *A Theology of Liberation*[10] marked a milestone, establishing a framework for ongoing theological reflection on the relation between the gospel message of salvation and the process of human liberation from the express viewpoint of the poor. The goal of liberation theology was recognized and explicitly stated in terms of being effective good news for the poor. A theology in Latin America simply had to be a theology of liberation. In fact, only as a liberating force could it now be theology at all. With great confidence, this new direction in theology appeals to a firm scriptural base in the historical praxis of Jesus himself, born into a situation of poverty, living in solidarity with the poor, and proclaiming the good news to them.[11] As mediator of the Reign of God, Jesus liberates the poor, the oppressed, and the marginalized. His proclamation of the reign of God is preferentially directed to the outcast and downtrodden. The very heart of his teaching is that the liberation of the enslaved is the manifestation of the God who reigns to give life and freedom.

A Latin American Liberation Trinitarian Theology— Leonardo Boff's *Trinity and Society*

In terms of trinitarian theology, the critical question for liberation theology must be: In what way is trinitarian theology good news for the poor in their lived experience? Here we turn to the work of Brazilian liberation theologian Leonardo Boff who has undertaken a sustained exploration of the doctrine of the Trinity, seeking practical expression of the doctrine for the advancement of human dignity, especially for the poor. As he explains: "If the Trinity is good news, then it is so particularly for the oppressed and those condemned to solitude."[12]

Boff recognizes that trinitarian faith can be liberating to those who are oppressed and marginalized insofar as it locates the root and prototype of human communion, and ultimately universal communion, in this mystery of the trinitarian communion. This is how it is good news for the poor, oppressed and marginalized, for in this way the sense of social belonging and of hope for the future is grounded in the triune God, a community of equals. As Boff explains, "...[t]he communion of the Trinity is then their source of inspiration, plays a part in their protest, is a paradigm of what they are building."[13] Boff is understandably critical of classical trinitarian theology to the degree that it tends to eclipse the social dimension of trinitarian mystery. He finds the concept of the monarchy of the Father particularly problematic, because the notions of divine monotheism and paternalism, based on the monarchy of the Father, have effectively functioned to legitimate the totalitarian structures that have been so oppressive and exploitative of the poor.

By elaborating a distinctly social model of the Trinity, Boff is able to situate the communion of the Trinity at the foundation of social and integral liberation. The liberating potential of trinitarian faith lies precisely in the fact that God is not the solitude of the solitary One, but a communion in love of three distinct divine persons. The Trinity is a mystery of relationships existing among divine coequals. Furthermore, on the basis of an understanding of God as communion, the oppressive structures which have so humiliated the poor can be more clearly identified and rejected.

Boff's reflections on the trinitarian communion of distinct coequal divine persons produces a critical attitude to the notions of personhood and community, in society and in the church. Given the dehumanizing and depersonalizing situation of the multitudes of the poor in Latin America, the trinitarian concept of person is a particularly crucial one in Boff's liberation trinitarian theology. Similarly, the categories of communion and of relationship, as realized in the divine life, emerge as powerful categories for a critique of the prevailing individualism and social disintegration within the culture, and as critical concepts by which the liberating power of trinitarian faith is reclaimed. Boff observes, for example, that only persons can be in communion. To be in communion is to be in loving and life-giving interpersonal relationships of radical reciprocity and mutuality, of mutual giving and receiving. Boff writes: "Life is the essence of God. And life is communion given and received. This kind of communion is love. Communion and love are the essence of God the Trinity."[14] In the Trinity, each of the divine persons exists in, with, and for the others in a communion of life and love.

The term *perichoresis* is a particularly evocative trinitarian notion, almost emblematic of liberation trinitarian theology. It describes the nature of this mystery of communion of love as so complete that each of the divine persons interpenetrates the others. As Boff explains:

> In my view, the perichoresis-communion model seems to be the most adequate way of expressing revelation of the Trinity as communicated and witnessed by the scriptures. Seen within the framework of perichoresis, the theories elaborated by theology and the church to signify the Christian God as person, relationship, divine nature and procession, are not invalidated, but become comprehensible.[15]

The Trinity is manifestly a mystery of inclusion and participation. So, too, the mysteries of creation and redemption, for the Holy Spirit and the Son are sent that all creation may participate in the trinitarian communion. The divine perichoresis clearly precludes any elevation or subordination of one person relative to another. Each divine person exists in relationships of equality, mutuality, and reciprocity. So it is that the model of the divine perichoresis serves as a source of inspiration for the human community of relationships. As Boff observes:

> Oppressed Christians find an incomparable inspiration for the liberation struggle in the God of their faith. This liberation aims to bring about participation and communion, the realities that most closely mirror the very mystery of trinitarian communion in human history.[16]

Since God is a perichoretic community of divine persons, then sovereignty is to be understood not in terms of power over the other but as communion, coexistence with others, in fellowship and *koinōnia*. The Trinity, understood in this way, is no abstract doctrine but a radical social program, serving as criticism of and inspiration for human society.[17] It is the paradigm for human community and social structure. A society that is to be a sign and sacrament of the Trinity will be a society that is based on relationships of equality, participation, inclusion and communion.

> The domination model is replaced by the communion model: production by invitation, conquest by participation. The Trinity understood in human terms as a communion of Persons lays the foundations for a society of brothers and sisters, of equals, in which dialogue and consensus are the basic constituents of living together in both the world and the church.[18]

For Boff, this understanding of the Trinity is abundantly rich in its suggestion for human community, particularly in relation to situations where there is little sharing, failure in communion, a great weight of oppression on the poor, and longing for liberation. It both justifies and inspires the struggle for more equitable and egalitarian political structures. It also demands respect for difference and diversity among people and groups, for only such a social organization faithfully accords with this understanding of the triune God. Boff explains:

This is where faith in the Holy Trinity, in the mystery of perichoresis, of the trinitarian communion and divine society, takes on a special resonance, since the Trinity can be seen as a model for any just, egalitarian (while respecting differences) social organization. On the basis of their faith in the triune God, Christians postulate a society that can be the image and likeness of the Trinity. Faith in the Trinity of Persons, Father, Son and Holy Spirit, can be seen to offer a response to the great quest for participation, equality and communion that fires the understanding of the oppressed. Both on the lowest levels of society and in the church there is a rejection of the exclusive type of society under which we all suffer to a greater or lesser extent.[19]

From the perspective of liberation theology, the trinitarian community of Father, Son, and Holy Spirit becomes the "prototype of the human community."[20] The goal is therefore to build a society which is in the image and likeness of the Trinity. If the human person really is the *imago Dei, the imago trinitatis,* then there must be a *vestigium trinitatis* in any human society deriving from the divine society which the Trinity is.[21] Human community should model trinitarian community and the divine perichoresis. It should be a community of inclusion, characterized by unity and diversity, and unity in diversity. Only a church or a society that is structured on such lines is genuinely a sacrament of the Trinity. As Boff notes:

> The sort of society that would emerge from inspiration by the trinitarian model would be one of fellowship, equality of opportunity, generosity in the space available for personal and group expression. Only a society of sisters and brothers whose social fabric is woven out of participation and communion of all in everything can justifiably claim to be an image and likeness (albeit pale) of the Trinity, the foundation and final resting-place of the universe.[22]

A great change in individual and social reality and distribution of power is clearly required if human reality is genuinely to image the trinitarian mystery. Here are the trinitarian roots of a commitment to transformation of society, to the liberation of the oppressed, and to the cause of social justice, which Boff expresses in the lapidary statement: "The holy Trinity is our social program."[23]

A critique of social systems necessarily follows from this understanding of the dynamic trinitarian perichoresis. The trinitarian communion challenges both capitalism and socialism, as well as individualism. On the one hand, the capitalist system promotes domination based on the One, and correspondingly the concentration of power in one person/group/elite, with a consequent marginalization of the majority. Goods are privately appropriated. Individual differences and development are valued to the detriment of communion. Averse to equal and equitable participation, capitalist regimes are clearly antithetical to trinitarian life. On the other hand, the socialist system, while emphasizing the principle of universal participation, devalues personal differences and the person as such. It tends to dismiss the value of individuals, subsuming them into a homogenizing and egalitarian whole, failing to see them as different-in-relation. It does not safeguard differences, and lacks respect for differences between persons and communities. It tends to impose its socialist program from above, by bureaucratic means, through the party which sees itself as the vanguard of social revolution and the interpreter of history. There is not a full realization and appreciation of the social dimension, starting at base and involving personal relationships that a genuinely trinitarian social program demands. In contrast to both of these social systems, the trinitarian mystery of God inspires social forms that foster a truly egalitarian familial community wherein individual differences are valued and safeguarded, and which is characterized by inclusion and participation.

From this perspective, a liberationist trinitarian theology challenges not only social organization but ecclesial organization as well. Boff explains:

The solar mystery of perichoretic communion in the Trinity
sheds light on the lunar mystery of the church. This is a
"derived mystery" (*mysterium derivatum*, an expression
used by the Fathers), derived from other more basic mysteries and in particular that of love and communion between the
three divine Persons. Just as there is trinitarian *koinōnia*, so
there is ecclesial *koinōnia*. The main definition of the church
is this: the community of the faithful in communion with the
Father, through the incarnate Son, in the Holy Spirit, and in
communion with each other and with their leaders.[24]

Based on his understanding of the trinitarian communion,
Boff is critical of the organization of the Roman Catholic
Church. He sees its present hierarchical-monarchical structure as
antithetical to collegiality, as allowing for, if not promoting,
inequality in the community, and the corresponding concentration of power in the clerical class or corps with little differentiated participation in the community. It too easily permits
paternalistic/authoritarian attitudes, as exemplified in its system
of canonical penalties for those who fail to submit to ecclesiasti-
cal authority. The trinitarian communion subverts such a sys
temic concentration of power, however, and demands the
flexibility of a broad egalitarian participation of all.

> The trinitarian vision produces a vision of a church that is
> more communion than hierarchy, more service than power,
> more circular than pyramidal, more loving embrace than
> bending the knee before authority. Such a perichoretic
> model of the church would submit all ecclesial functions
> (episcopate, presbyterate, lay ministries, and so on) to the
> imperative of communion and participation by all in every-
> thing that concerns the good of all.[25]

In this way, liberation theology's understanding of the mystery of the Trinity challenges us, as the *communitas fidelium,* to a
model of church that is characterized by relationships of equality.
Only thus, as a community of coequals, is the church a sign of the

Trinity. Only thus is she able to be sacrament of the Trinity. Boff
writes:

> The model of a truly liberated church, one that could serve
> as a model for liberation, can be projected from the mystery
> of the communion between the three divine Persons....
> Such a church, inspired by the communion of the Trinity,
> would be characterized by a more equitable sharing of
> sacred power, by dialogue, by openness to all the charisms
> granted to the members of the community, by the disappear-
> ance of all types of discrimination, especially those originat-
> ing in patriarchalism and *machismo,* by its permanent
> search for all consensus to be built up through the organized
> participation of all its members.[26]

For liberation theology, trinitarian faith is not just an issue
of orthodoxy but of orthopraxis. Such a liberating praxis is related
to the reign of God in the conviction that this reign is to be built up
in the actual historical reality of faith's experience. It is not to be
dismissed as ideological and Marxist, since faith in the Trinity
demands the criticism of all social injustices and a commitment to
social transformation. Boff's liberation trinitarian theology, therefore, makes a clear link between trinitarian theology and political
theology by recognizing the trinitarian communion as a critical
source of inspiration for social and ecclesial structural changes. It
recognizes that the liberating character of God's trinitarian and
social character demands a political theory which insists on social
interaction, inclusion and participation, a human community of
shared participation and responsibility without subordination or
marginalization.

Given that the specifically social dimension of trinitarian
theology is critical to Boff, it is hardly surprising that his treatment of each of the three divine persons is relatively brief. Each is
described under the rubric of liberation. Interestingly, and perhaps somewhat ironically given his criticism of classical trinitarian theology, and particularly the notion of the monarchy of the

Father, Boff adopts the traditional order of approach to the divine persons and begins his elaboration of the trinitarian symbol with a treatment of the person of the Father.

The Father—Origin and Goal of All Liberation[27]

It is in the name of the Father that Jesus the Son liberates the oppressed. Jesus proclaims the kingdom of his Father. But it is not a kingdom in the style of earthly kingdoms, based on concentration of power in the hands of a few. God the Father is definitely not the Great Father, the supreme authority of the universe, from whom all other religious and civil authorities derive their authority, in descending orders of hierarchy. The kingdom which Jesus proclaims is the kingdom of goodness and mercy, wherein the humble are exalted. This is how and why the gospel is good news for the poor.

The Father is the father of Jesus, the Father who sends his Son in order that all creation might share in the divine communion and fellowship of life and love. Creation is the fruit of their love. It is "an expression of the intimate, perichoretic life of God, a life that expands outwards, creating different beings with whom God can communicate and enter into communion."[28] The trinitarian perichoretic setting of the divine fatherhood strongly challenges any notion of a patriarchal father and any social or political structure based on authoritarianism, paternalism, and patriarchalism—those very structures which have oppressed the poor throughout history. The Father is Father, not in solitary and unique splendor, and not as the supreme authority of the universe from whom all other authorities derive. To the contrary, the Father is never Father without the Son; nor, in our actual experience, without his adopted sons and daughters in the Son. After the resurrection, Jesus calls his disciples "my brothers" and the Father "my Father and your Father" (Jn 20:17). The fatherhood of the

Father is the basis of that universal fellowship that constitutes human community as a society of coequal brothers and sisters.

As the God of liberation, the Father hears the cries of the poor and downtrodden and desires the liberation of the oppressed. "This Father-God, far from being paternalistic, sends his children, as he sent his Son Jesus, to shake off their fetters and take their proper task in hand, building up the Kingdom of freedom of his sons and daughters."[29] Moreover, Boff explains that the first person is Mother as well as Father.[30] Both analogies are necessary, he argues, to attempt to convey the richness of the first person of the Trinity.

The Son—The Mediator of Liberation[31]

As Son, Jesus calls God "Father." He reveals the character of his Father whose love extends to all men and women, but especially to outcasts and sinners, the poor and the oppressed, and ultimately to all creation. Jesus, the incarnate Son, is mediator and executor of the Father's plan. In this regard, he embodies the liberating intention of God in carrying out the Father's mission. In the person of Jesus, Boff also recognizes the freedom of sonship, a freedom which Jesus passes on to others—in his teaching, his miracles, and the forgiveness of sins in the Father's name, freeing the poor from legalism and injustice.

Boff also identifies a feminine dimension in Jesus, the Son.[32] He writes:

> This feminine dimension belongs to the humanity of Jesus, hypostatically taken on by the eternal Son. Femininity thereby strikes roots into the very heart of the mystery of God. Though Jesus was a man and not a woman, the feminine dimension in him is equally divinized, revealing the maternal face of God.[33]

The Holy Spirit—The Divine Force of Liberation[34]

Having identified a feminine dimension in both Father and Son, Boff also identifies the feminine dimension of the Holy Spirit.[35] But here he adds a note of caution:

> We need to remind ourselves that God is beyond sex... In other words, by saying that each of the Persons contains masculine and feminine dimensions, we are not conferring sexual characteristics on the mystery of the Trinity, or trying to find them in it. What we are trying to do is discern the ultimate source of the values the Trinity itself has conferred on human beings in their masculine and feminine embodiments. Through being beyond human sexes, the Trinity embraces the dimensions of the feminine and the masculine in all their mystery insofar as those dimensions are image and likeness of the source of all existence, the most Holy Trinity itself.[36]

Boff, together with other liberation theologians, finds in the Holy Spirit the power of the new and of a renewal in all things: "It would seem as though the Spirit follows the logic of imagination and its wonderful constructs, against the power of established facts."[37] Moreover, the Holy Spirit is the spirit of liberation, for where there is the Spirit, there is freedom; and where there is freedom, there is difference, because of the variety of spiritual gifts. As the power of union within all beings, the Holy Spirit prevents differences from degenerating into inequalities and discrimination. Instead, the Spirit maintains all in communion, as the gift of love uniting all creation. The Holy Spirit creates and sustains both difference and communion. Indeed, the presence of the Spirit is indicated precisely by the presence of a rich and lively diversity of gifts and services in a community. Unity, not uniformity, is the hallmark of the Holy Spirit.

The Spirit is the spirit of new creation, of creativity, animation, and innovation, though never in an individualistic manner, but always for the building up of the community. The mission of the Holy Spirit yields diversity and communion, action and transformation. The Holy Spirit liberates from oppression; it is the catalyst of liberation. As Boff explains:

> When the poor become conscious of their oppression, come together, organize their forces, throw over the taboos that held them in subjection, unmask the standards by which they were stigmatized, prophetically denounce those who kept them in chains; when, obliged to use force they did not want to, they face up to the violence of their oppressors and strip them of their privileges and unjust rank; when they are filled with creative imagination and plan utopias of the reconciled world in which all will have enough to eat and be able to profit from the bounty of nature, then we can say: the Spirit is at work there, being the catalyst in a conflictive situation. Such historical processes are pregnant with the Spirit.[38]

From the perspective of Latin American liberation theology, as exemplified in the work of Leonardo Boff, the mystery of the Trinity emerges with remarkable power as inspiration, as critic, and as fully and actively present in the struggles of the oppressed for liberation. Admittedly, we find in Boff's work not so much a critique of classical trinitarian theology, but a critique of Latin American society and of the ecclesial forms of the church in that society in the light of the social model of Trinity. In terms of trinitarian theology as such, we find no major reconstruction of the classical trinitarian notions, but rather a reclamation, with particular emphasis on the social dimension in trinitarian theology and its radical and fundamentally world-shattering ramifications for human society. What is highly significant is that, in Latin American liberation theology, trinitarian orthodoxy finds cogent and potent expression in a trinitarian orthopraxis. It is a theology which insists on the translation of doctrine into praxis. It expressly intends to make a social difference, in both the practice of the church and in the structure of society. In other words, it is a theology of praxis, a theologically-inspired "conduct" rather than an academically-produced "product." The classical understanding of theology as *fides quaerens intellectum*, faith seeking understanding, yields to *fides quaerens justitiam et libertatem*, faith seeking justice and liberty.

3
The Trinity and Christian Feminist Liberation Theologies

Classical Christian theology has always held that the ineffable mystery of God remains unutterably beyond human comprehension, concepts, and images. However, in practice, Christian theology has made overwhelming use of male imagery and names to designate the divinity. God is effectively identified as male, certainly far more male than female, and moreover in such powerful and pervasive ways that male imagery for the divine tends to perdure even when gender-neutral imagery is explicitly engaged. Feminist theology emerges precisely in reaction to this distortion and takes up a critique of the androcentric bias of theology, whereby God is imaged as male, where male experience is assumed to be normative for human experience, where women are excluded from the sacramental system and from ecclesial decision making, and structures of dualism leave women subordinate to men, marginalized, and excluded. It challenges the church to examine its use of language and images, its policies and practices, and to expunge all that is demeaning and destructive of the full humanity of women.

We should note, however, that the term "feminist" is somewhat problematic these days, for there is vast diversity within contemporary feminism. We should strictly speak of feminist theologies, as distinct from feminist theology. But, for our purposes

here, suffice it to say that feminist theology is that field of theological endeavor which is concerned to expose and to redress the
patriarchal nature of traditional religions.[39] It is grounded in
women's experience of oppression, in society generally, and in
the church in particular. It embraces an alternative vision of
humanity wherein women and men are coequal in dignity and in
discipleship and where human community is based on genuine
mutuality and inclusion. At root, it is concerned for justice and
emancipation. To achieve its goal, feminist theology actively
seeks a reclamation of the feminine into theology, including a
reclamation of the knowledge and contributions of women that
have been lost or trivialized in the tradition. It purposefully
engages reflection on women's experience, in all its diversity and
particularity, in a determined effort to unmask and deconstruct the
language, structures, institutions, and symbol systems that perpet-
uate patriarchy and the institutional and structural domination of
women by men.

A Feminist Reconstruction of Trinitarian Theology— Elizabeth Johnson's *She Who Is*

Theological feminism is particularly critical of masculinist
conceptions of the divine. Here it recognizes that religion perpet-
uates patriarchy to the degree that it masculinizes God and con-
ceives of God's relationship to the world as analogous to man's
relationship to woman.

The point is, as Mary Daly expresses it so pungently, "if
God is male, then the male is God."[40] If God is male, then the
female is evidently not fully in the image of God; she is "not
God." Yet neither scriptures nor the theological tradition support
the exclusive application of male images and names to God. In
fact, the Fourth Lateran Council in 1215 definitively expressed
the necessary but limited nature of our language about God in

terms of there being a greater dissimilarity than similarity between Creator and creature.[41] But as Johnson explains:

> We have forgotten what was clear to early Christian thinkers, namely, that Father and Son are names that designate relationship rather than an essence in itself, and that as applied to God they, like all human finite names, are subject to the negation of the rule of analogy.[42]

Clearly, the symbol of God as the ultimate symbol of a whole religious system is a crucial one. It functions to shape the associated language and symbol systems of the community, determines not only doctrine but praxis, and molds the identity of the community, corporately and individually. However, the naming of God in feminist terms remains problematic. The great preponderance of male imagery and names for the divine in scriptures, liturgy, and art effectively combine to stymie the feminist liberation project. Hence the claim of the post-Christian feminists that Christianity is irredeemably patriarchal and androcentric, hopelessly beyond retrieval.

North American theologian Elizabeth Johnson takes a different tack and opts for a retrieval of the tradition. In her work, *She Who Is,* we find a remarkably fine example of a feminist critical retrieval of trinitarian theology, based on a rich reclamation of the biblical image of Sophia for language about God. "The symbol of God functions," as Johnson says.[43] In the classical tradition of trinitarian theology, it functions to exclude and oppress women. In Johnson's theology, it functions in a radically new way that is liberating for women.

For Johnson, a thorough analysis of sexism as it affects the tradition is a vital step toward a genuine retrieval of the doctrine of God. A hermeneutic of suspicion demands that one search for the biases at work in any system or tradition—in this case, biases that operate to obliterate the incorporation of the feminine into our God-talk. As Bernard Lonergan recognized, just as insight can be desired, so too it can be unwanted. There can occur a hardening of the mind to unwanted wisdom, the refusal of insight, an intellectual censorship, a blind spot for insight.[44]

Johnson offers an insightful analysis of traditional trinitarian theology, examining the blind spots that are the legacy of sexism. She identifies the effects of sexism within society generally and in theological discourse specifically, then focuses directly on the debilitating effects of patriarchal names, imagery, and structure of the Trinity on the Christian community, and on women in particular. She concludes that women "have been consistently defined as mentally, morally, and physically inferior to men, created only partially in the image of God, even a degrading symbol of evil.... Their femaleness is judged to be not suitable as metaphor for speech about God."[45] On these grounds, she argues that the doctrine of the Trinity, when distorted by sexism, actually became subversive of the good news of the rule of God which Jesus proclaimed. Johnson identifies the primary problem as the virtually exclusive use of male imagery. "The evocative power of the deeply masculinized symbol of the Trinity points implicitly to an essential divine maleness, inimical to women's being *imago Dei* precisely as female."[46] Wittingly or unwittingly, the use of male imagery for the divine effectively undermines, excludes, and dehumanizes women.

Johnson recognizes that the classical form of trinitarian theology effectively legitimates patriarchal subordination through its use of male imagery and its portrayal of a monarchical image of God and a divine hierarchical pattern of relationships. She also recognizes an implicit subordination in the Trinity of divine persons, for processions necessarily imply rank. The second and third divine persons, in some sense at least, are not genuinely and equally persons in the way that the first is. Both originate from the first person, who is the apex of the Trinity, the font of divinity. As Johnson writes:

> When the model used...focuses on the procession of the
> first to second to third, a subtle hierarchy is set up and, like a

drowned continent, bends all currents of trinitarian thought
to the shape of the model used. Through insistence on the
right order of certain processions, ontological priority
inevitably ends up with the Father while at the other end of
the processions the Spirit barely trails along.[47]

The traditional trinitarian model is all too clearly coherent with
patriarchal structures in church and society. It functions to legitimate the hierarchical ordering of society and church, the subjugation of women and, moreover, the subjugation of creation
generally. It makes man-father the divinely ordained head of fam-
ily, household, church, and state. In this way, as Johnson argues,
sexism within theological discourse has actually subverted trinitarian theology, rendering the symbol in such a way as to be
destructive of the full humanity of persons, male and female.
Clearly, very different metaphor systems are needed to show
mutuality, equality, and reciprocal dynamism of trinitarian relations. On the other hand, the mutual relationship that lies at the
very heart of the classical doctrine of the Trinity has strong affini-
ties with feminist values of relationality, mutuality, friendship, and
equality, as well as complementarity and community in diversity.

Johnson proposes that a reconstruction of trinitarian imagery
is imperative, for the Father-Son analogy as a primary mode of
expression has effectively legitimated a social world based on hierarchy and inequality between men and women. Johnson therefore
embarks on a reconstruction of doctrine of the Trinity intentionally
using only female metaphors for, as she explains,

only if the full reality of woman as well as man enters into
the conceptualization of God, can the idolatrous fixation on
one image be broken and the truth of the mystery of God, in
tandem with the liberation of human beings in all of our
mystery, emerge for all time.[48]

Johnson returns to the biblical sources and, in the image of
God as *Sophia* and in the tradition of wisdom theology and

Christology, locates a rich resource for a retrieval of trinitarian theology which is able to meet the feminist critique of traditional trinitarian theology. In the image of God as *Sophia*, Holy Wisdom, she finds a powerful and evocative vehicle for expressing God's threefold creative, saving, and sanctifying action in the world which readily lends itself to a female imaging of the Trinity. She proceeds to articulate the threefold aspects of encounter with the Trinity in terms of Spirit-Sophia, Jesus-Sophia, and Mother-Sophia. She begins her treatment of the three divine persons with the Holy Spirit.

Spirit-Sophia[49]

Johnson, in a counter to the traditional approach of trinitarian theology which begins a treatment of the three divine persons with the person of the Father as font of the divinity, in fact begins with a consideration of the Spirit. She notes the striking affinity between language about the Spirit— as freely moving, life-giving, nonviolent, as the power that connects, renews, and blesses—and feminist values and leitmotifs.

The whole universe comes into being and remains in being through divine creative power, *Creator Spiritus*. She is the giver of life, the vivifier. The Spirit is both the source of individuation and of community, of autonomy and of relation. She vivifies, knits together, and upholds creation in a pervading and unquenchable liberating love. Thanks to her presence, all creation is mutually related, existing in an interplay of communion. Connectedness is the mark of her presence.

Spirit-Sophia is source of renewal and of transformation. She initiates the new. She transforms, renews, and recreates. She inspires creativity and joy. She brings healing and liberation to brokenness and sin. Like a midwife (Ps 22:9–10), she brings life through pain and struggle. She is Spirit of healing, of transformation, and of liberation. She is there in the praxis of freedom. Like a bakerwoman, she keeps on kneading the leaven of kindness and truth, justice and peace into the dough of the world until the loaf rises (Mt 13:33).

She is also Spirit of renewal. To the discouraged, jaded, broken, exhausted, suffering, she brings healing, new life, and renewed hope and enthusiasm. Where there was a heart of stone, She creates a clean heart, a heart of compassion (Ez 36:26). She is the Spirit of forgiveness and reconciliation. She builds community. She is the gracious giver of gifts: love, joy, peace, patience, kindness, goodness, faithfulness, gentleness, and self-control.

The notion in traditional trinitarian theology that the Spirit is the power of mutual love of Father and Son, Spirit of their creative dynamic mutual love, bears a strong affinity with the model of relationship so highly prized by feminists. As the Spirit of mutual love, of love among equals, She cannot be used to legitimize patriarchal or hierarchical structures. To the contrary, this trinitarian imagery signals mutuality and reciprocity in community as the highest good.

In her portrayal of the image of Spirit-Sophia, Johnson subverts the dominance that is inherent in the patriarchal image of the Trinity which is so detrimental to our understanding of the mystery of God and, consequently, to human community. She engages three key insights of critical concern to feminist theology. First, Spirit Sophia, as the living God at her closest to the world—pervading, animating, and quickening the world, both differentiating and uniting—expresses the immanence of the transcendent God. Second, Spirit-Sophia, as spirit of freedom, as the power of healing and of liberation from whatever does not give life, expresses the divine passion for liberation. Third, Spirit-Sophia discloses the constitutive nature of relation, for it is impossible to speak of the Spirit-Sophia, either *ad intra* or *ad extra,* except in terms of relation. Relationality is intrinsic to her being as gift, love, life. In this thought-provoking way, Johnson sets biblical and classical teaching on the Spirit in spirited dialogue with the insights of feminist

theology. The extraordinary novelty of her approach, the fundamental *raison-d'être* of her method, is that it paves the way to recognizing women as *imago Dei*.

Jesus-Sophia[50]

We find even greater novelty and ingenuity as Johnson
applies female imagery to Jesus, using the female image of personified Wisdom to articulate the mystery of Jesus the Christ. Her
project is the same—to show that woman is truly and equally
imago Dei—but here Johnson must contend with the historical
fact of Jesus' maleness. Here is a very critical point for her argument, for Jesus' maleness has been used as a sacred justification
for male dominance and female subordination, having been
claimed to be essential to his redeeming christic function and
identity. Johnson's project is therefore to effect a retrieval of
Jesus' profound relatedness to God's own being and to all human
beings, but without signifying the maleness, because that is the
problem endemic in the traditional metaphors, Word and Son.
This then is the significance of Johnson's use of the intentionally
female image of Jesus-Sophia in her feminist reconstruction of
trinitarian theology.

Johnson proceeds to describe Jesus in terms of *Sophia* incarnate, the Wisdom of God, the prophet of God sent to announce
that God is the God of all-inclusive love who wills the wholeness
and humanity of everyone, but most especially the poor and marginalized. In Jesus' teaching, in his ministry of healing, and in his
table community that is scandalously inclusive of all, Jesus attests
the reality of the ever gracious goodness and renewing power of
Sophia-God drawing near. He addresses her as Abba. He variously likens her to a shepherd who has lost his sheep, a woman
looking for a lost coin, a father forgiving a wayward son, a mother
giving birth. In these ways, Jesus-Sophia unleashes a hope that is
grounded in a vision of a community of equals, a community

based on liberating relationships that are characterized by mutual respect, compassion, comfort, support, and forgiveness—a community that is based on relationships of friendship as distinct from patterns of domination-subordination.

Jesus-Sophia is crucified, betrayed by his friends. Crucified, Jesus-Sophia rises, manifesting the truth that divine justice and power leavens the world in quite different ways than those of dominating violence. Ultimately, the cross itself raises a profound challenge to any sense of the natural rightness of male dominating rule, for it embodies the very opposite of the patriarchal ideal of the powerful man, evidence rather of the steep price that is to be paid in the struggle for liberation. The cross is clearly part of the painful pathway to life, just as birth is the painful and life-threatening passage from the womb. The resurrection witnesses Sophia's characteristic gift of life: life is given anew and in abundance, in unimaginable ways. The Spirit is lavishly poured out on the disciples and they, men and women alike, are commissioned to go out and spread the good news.

Jesus-Sophia, Sophia incarnate, concretely embodied, connects God for all eternity to the world, to its suffering and delight, to compassion and liberation. Long held dichotomies, such as body/spirit, creator/creature, male/female are overturned. Herein lies the mystery of Jesus' identity as Christ; it does not reside in his maleness. In fact, Johnson argues that an androcentric stress on Jesus' maleness warrants the charge of heresy. Jesus' maleness is undeniably an aspect of his personal historical identity, but it is not theologically determinative of his identity as Christ. His maleness is simply and only a particularity. Johnson writes:

> Theology will have come of age when the particularity that is highlighted is not Jesus' historical sex but the scandal of his option for the poor and marginalized in the Spirit of his compassionate, liberating Sophia-God. That is the scandal of particularity that really matters, aimed as it is toward the creation of a new order of wholeness in justice. Toward that

end, feminist theological speech about Jesus the Wisdom of God shifts the focus of reflection off maleness and onto the whole theological significance of what transpires in the Christ event. Jesus in his human, historical specificity is confessed as Sophia incarnate, revelatory of the liberating graciousness of God images as female; women, as friends of Jesus-Sophia, share equally with men in his saving mission throughout time and can fully represent Christ, being themselves in the Spirit, other Christs. These are steps on the way to a community of equals in genuine mutuality, in theory as well as practice.[51]

Understood in this light, the doctrine of the incarnation also sounds a ringing affirmation of another treasured feminist leitmotif, the value of bodiliness, even for God. It evinces the transcendent God's capacity for bodiliness.[52]

We see then how Johnson, by engaging the female figure of personified Wisdom to speak about Jesus the Christ, offers a much augmented field of metaphors with which to interpret his saving significance, in ways that escape the dominant male images of Logos and Son.

Mother-Sophia[53]

The hidden God is known three-fold: as Spirit-Sophia, who pervades the world to vivify and renew; in the person of Jesus-Sophia, Sophia incarnate, who heals, redeems and liberates; and third as absolute mystery, unoriginate origin and goal of all creation, whose character Jesus-Sophia reveals as one of infinite graciousness, compassion, and love, most especially for the poor and the outcast.

Continuing her project to construct a trinitarian theology on the basis of female imagery, Johnson recognizes mothering as a most apt metaphor to express God as creator of heaven and earth, of all that is seen and unseen. The language of God as mother expresses, in a preeminent way, the mystery of creation, genera-tion, and care. To speak of God as mother is to express God as unoriginate origin, primordial being, hidden source of all that is, creator, source of life. Johnson explains:

> Maternity with its creativity, nurturing, and warmth, its unbounded compassion and concern for justice, its sover-eign power that protects, heals, and liberates, its all-embracing immanence, and its recreative energy shapes a new understanding of divine relationality, mystery, and liberating intent.[54]

Note that in this image of God as Mother-Sophia, the divine com-passion is also strongly allied with a concern for justice. Mother-Sophia creates and sustains all and rejoices in its flourishing. Her power is the power of love, life, and liberation. Her preferential love is for the weak, the dispossessed, the poor, and the lost.

The mother metaphor points powerfully to an intrinsic related-ness between God and the world, a notion that is far removed from the classical understanding, so often misunderstood and misinter-preted, that God has no real relation to the world. The image of Mother-Sophia, in contrast, clearly bespeaks an intimate connected-ness. All creatures exist in relations of mutual kinship with each other and with God their mother, creator of heaven and earth, who delights in creation and whose passion it is to bring the whole world to the fullness of life in justice, peace, and universal harmony.

With her treatment of Mother-Sophia, Johnson completes her triune symbol, depicted in deliberately female metaphors, of the trinitarian pattern of our experience of God. Johnson then takes up the metaphor of *friendship* as a model for trinitarian rela-tionships.[55] Instead of the classical model of relations of origin, she explains the profound mystery of relatedness within the Trin-ity in terms of the mutuality of friendship. Modelling the triune symbol on relations of friendship and describing it in wisdom metaphors results in a trinitarian theology that is characterized by mutuality, relation, equality, and community in diversity and which, as such, offers an alternative to the male imagery of the classical model and the hierarchical pattern of relationship that frequently, albeit subtly, attends it.

Johnson finally turns to the biblical tetragrammaton, YHWH, God's self-identifying name given to Moses at the burning bush (Ez 3:14). Although virtually untranslatable it has traditionally been rendered as "I am who I am" or "I am" and, understandably, became linked in the theological tradition with the metaphysical notion of being. Aquinas draws on this tradition when he describes the divine mystery in terms of being itself and the divine essence as identical with divine existence. *Ergo hoc nomen, "qui est," est maxime proprium nomen Dei,* Aquinas concludes.[56] But, in Johnson's hands, Aquinas's *qui est* becomes not He Who Is, but She Who Is. Johnson argues that, if God is not intrinsically male, if women are truly created in the image of God, then there is cogent reason to name Sophia-God "the one who is," the one whose very nature is sheer and exuberant aliveness, the profoundly relational source of being, wellspring of life, dynamic act, She Who Is. As Johnson explains:

> SHE WHO IS: linguistically this is possible; theologically it is legitimate; existentially and religiously it is necessary if speech about God is to shake off the shackles of idolatry and be a blessing for women. In the present sexist situation where structures and language, praxis and personal attitudes convey an ontology of inferiority to women, naming toward God in this way is a gleam of light on the road to genuine community.[57]

In this powerful, even startling, way, Elizabeth Johnson achieves her goal: women's human nature is disclosed as *imago Dei*. Thus is the very linchpin of patriarchy, a masculinist conception of God, removed, and also every structure and attitude that would assign superiority to men on the basis of their supposedly greater godlikeness invalidated. There is perhaps a sense of shock for the reader in Johnson's lapidary expression, She Who Is. That

Johnson's proposal is somewhat strange and even shocking only further serves to highlight just how very deeply masculinist conceptions of the divinity have come to permeate our thinking and our imagination.

We see then that Johnson pushes further than Boff. Boff takes classical trinitarian theology and shows that its understanding of the godhead as a Trinity of three coequal divine persons in a community of love has powerful ramifications for human society. Johnson's feminist liberation theology pushes further still, for she recognizes that the rhetoric and symbolism of the classical form of trinitarian theology is itself masculinist in construction and, as such, distorted in its representation of the godhead. Johnson thus offers a bracing challenge to trinitarian theology. Her extraordinary achievement is not to be dismissed lightly. This critical retrieval of trinitarian theology is thoroughly steeped in the theological tradition, profoundly respectful of it, incisive in its assessment, carefully measured in its judgment, yet daring and determined in its challenge to the tradition. It deserves our best attention and constructive response.

4
Ecological Approaches to the Trinity

There is little doubt that as a world community we are currently at a point of ecological crisis. Media reports frequently refer to it in various forms: the destruction of the environment and its ecosystems, exploitation of the earth's resources, damage to the ozone shield, pollution of the atmosphere and water systems, the degradation of the land, the destruction of wilderness areas, massive deforestation worldwide; the list goes on. This urgent sense of ecological crisis is matched by a growing consciousness of our cosmos as an evolutionary ecosystem and of the tremendous diversity of life in a biosphere of interconnected and interdependent living things. There is a newly emerging realization and appreciation of the relational aspect of all reality at both macro and micro empirical level, of interconnectedness and relationality as inherent to the entire universe. The prevailing paradigm of reality has clearly changed. In the classical tradition, the human self was understood in terms of matter and spirit and the divine image sought, by analogy, in the spiritual acts and capacities. In contrast, our modern scientific mind is increasingly conscious of the interrelatedness of the universe as a whole.

This crisis and this new consciousness offers a new challenge to theology. The situation calls for a fresh rethinking of the meaning of the Trinity "for us and our salvation." As Simone Weil comments, "How can Christianity call itself catholic if the universe itself is left out?"[58] The ability to rearticulate its beliefs in the light of contemporary issues and pastoral needs is one of the great strengths of Roman Catholic theology. There is the healthy and life-giving recognition that, after all, no theology can fully express, once and for all, the being of God and God's relationship to creation. It is therefore not surprising that theological responses to this distinctly ecological challenge are now beginning to emerge. We find that trinitarian theology is being reimagined and reconfigured in more distinctly relational terms and properly cosmic proportions.

Denis Edwards: Jesus, The Wisdom of God[59]

One effort to respond to the ecological challenge is that of Australian theologian Denis Edwards. In his work we find a new overture of trinitarian theology to the ecological reality of our planet. In fact, Edwards' work demonstrates just how very hospitable trinitarian thinking is to the ecological imagination.

Edwards argues, in the light of contemporary individualism and the ecological crisis, and alongside the theologies of Augustine and Aquinas, that we need to retrieve a distinctly communal model of the Trinity and to attend particularly and consistently to the trinitarian relations with creatures. He would persuade us that there is a profound link between an adequate theology and an ecological stance. Theology is necessarily ecological. Edwards presses further and argues that the central truths of Christian faith in fact push us beyond any kind of anthropocentrism to an ethic of intrinsic value. He then proceeds to build "an ecological theology which is radically theological in that it is based on a systematic understanding of the trinitarian God."[60] Wisdom Christology provides the foundation on which he develops this ecological understanding of the trinitarian God. It affords the necessary bridge between trinitarian theology, on the one hand, and the theology of human beings in relationship to other creatures, on the other.

Edwards' aim is clear. Convinced that trinitarian theology

and ecological theology necessarily converge, he intends what he himself describes as "an ecological *theology*."[61] He constructs an intentionally ecological theology of God, with a trinitarian theology of God's interaction with creation at its center. It is a trinitarian theology which springs from a Wisdom Christology and leads to ecologically-responsible praxis.

Edwards begins with an exploration of the biblical foundation on which to build an ecological Wisdom Christology. He observes that, in the biblical tradition of Wisdom literature, Wisdom is always closely associated with God's work of creation. Sophia, divine Wisdom personified in female terms, emerges as the one at work in all things—creating, sustaining, and redeeming. She is present with God at creation as a skilled coworker. She delights in all things and is revealed in all creatures. She renews all things. Wisdom is clearly concerned with the whole of creation and with the interrelationships among human beings, the rest of creation, and God. Edwards explains: "It is *this* Wisdom, radically associated with creation and with all creatures, who pitches a tent among us in the person of Jesus of Nazareth."[62]

With the biblical tradition of Wisdom literature at hand, the Christian tradition quickly identified Sophia and her cosmic role with Jesus Christ, with Wisdom categories readily lending themselves to an understanding of Jesus. Jesus is led by the Spirit. He relates to God as one possessed by the Spirit of God. He addresses God in intimate and familial terms as Abba. He shows God to be a God of radical compassion, a liberating and inclusive God, a God of intimate and familial relationships. Jesus is a great Wisdom teacher, speaking in the Wisdom categories of proverb and parable, confronting conventional wisdom and shattering the traditional taken-for-granted worldviews. His all-inclusive table fellowship echoes the bounteous banquet of the Wisdom Woman (Prv 9:3–5; Sir 24:19–21). His liberating and healing ministry anticipates the Reign of God (Lk 7:22), a God of boundless compassion and familial inclusiveness, a God whose preferential love is for the poor and the outcast. This application of Wisdom categories to Jesus, his teaching and his practice of feeding, healing, teaching, and liberating, together with the teaching of Wisdom Christologies of the Christian scriptures wherein Sophia is identified with Jesus, thus leads Edwards to a retrieval of Wisdom Christology and an understanding of Jesus as Wisdom incarnate, the Wisdom of God.

Jesus, the Wisdom of God, was rejected and crucified. Edwards recalls that, in Paul's theology, divine Wisdom is revealed most especially in the mystery of the cross. In Jesus, and in him crucified, God's loving Wisdom is revealed. The foolishness of God (1 Cor 1:25) is manifest as the foolishness of love beyond understanding; it is divine love revealed as compassionate, involved to a foolish excess in our struggle for life. Edwards argues that the identification between Wisdom and the cross has profound meaning for an ecological theology. It is *this* same Love that "moves the stars," as Dante recognized.[63]

The Trinitarian God and Creation

For a trinitarian theology, Edwards turns to the medieval theologians Richard of St. Victor and Bonaventure. Both stand in the tradition of Augustine, but each develops markedly different approaches to that of Thomas Aquinas. Richard of St. Victor develops a model of mutual love, while Bonaventure constructs a dynamic model of a self-expressive goodness wherein the universe is the self-expression of God. Here Edwards finds approaches to trinitarian theology that are congruent with the tradition of divine Wisdom and of Wisdom Christology and which can speak cogently to contemporary ecological issues.

The remarkable novelty of Richard of St. Victor's approach lies in the application of a reflection on Christian understanding of Christian friendship and love to the mystery of the Trinity. Unlike Aquinas, who takes up Augustine's psychological analogies,

Richard takes up Augustine's more social approach to the Trinity, the trinitarian model of the lover, the beloved, and their love. This marginal element in Augustine's approach becomes central in Richard's trinitarian theology and lays the foundation for a trinitarian theology which is quite different from that of Augustine's psychological theory of the Trinity.

Richard begins with an understanding of God as the fullness and perfection of all goodness. He then achieves a conjunction between the concept of God as perfect goodness and the New Testament concept of God as love. He argues that of all things that are good, nothing is better or more perfect than the fullness of love, which is charity. Richard concludes that charity is therefore the supreme content of the good. Since God is supreme goodness, such goodness must involve full and perfect self-transcending love and charity between persons. In this way, Richard concludes that there must necessarily be a plurality of persons in God. Further reflection on the human experience of happiness as involving mutual love supports Richard's first argument. Furthermore, given that it is the nature of divine glory to be benevolent in self-communication, there must be mutual giving of interpersonal self-communication in God. In other words, if God is abundantly good, happy, and glorious, then there must be self transcending love, real communication, and profound interrelationship and, therefore, a plurality of persons in God. Moreover, supreme charity demands that the love between the persons is not only mutual love but a love between equals. It therefore requires an equality of persons, an equality without any hint of subordination or hierarchy.

Charity, the supreme form of the good, thus becomes the basis for demonstrating that there must be a plurality of persons in the godhead. Richard's argument progresses from the fullness of divinity to the fullness of goodness to the fullness of charity to a plurality in God. Charity, which is the highest form of the good, necessarily requires a plurality in the godhead and Richard locates this plurality at the level of person. Further analysis leads to the conclusion that there must be not just two but at least three in this plurality, for if there were only two, then there could only be their love for one another, and not the fullness of love, which demands that the two persons share their love with another. As Richard explains:

> When one person gives love to another and…one loves only the other, there certainly is love *(dilectio)*, but it is not a shared love *(condilectio)*. When two love each other mutually *(mutuo diligent)* and give to each other the affection of supreme longing; when the affection of the first goes out to the second and the affection of the second goes out to the first and tends as it were in diverse ways—in this case there certainly is love *(dilectio)* on both sides, but it is not shared love *(condilectio)*. Shared love *(condilectio)* is properly said to exist when a third person is loved by two persons harmoniously *(concorditer diligitur)* and in community *(socialiter amatur)*, and the affection for the two persons is fused into one affection by the flame of love for the third.[64]

The third divine person emerges in Richard's trinitarian theology by reflection on the altruistic love of the lover and the beloved. Richard concludes that there must be not only the *dilectus* but the *condilectus* (the "loved with") as well.

Edwards also turns to Bonaventure's trinitarian theology. It is built on reflection on the first name of God as the Good (Lk 18:19), but also, in the tradition of Pseudo-Dionysius, on the understanding that goodness, by its very nature, is inherently self-communicative and self-diffusive *(bonum diffusivum sui)*. This latter notion serves as the metaphysical principle underlying Bonaventure's thought. We have noted that for Richard the principal argument for plurality of persons in God is drawn from an analysis of interpersonal love. However, for Bonaventure, "a mind well trained in the art of logic in a theologian who is all too often viewed only as a mystical theologian,"[65] the argument is carefully integrated into a metaphysics which is expressly based on the concept of the good. Trinitarian terminology, conditioned by the dynamics of fecundity, which plays no part in Richard's theology, thereby takes on a new meaning in Bonaventure's theology.

Bonaventure builds his trinitarian theology on the experience of God's action in the economy of salvation and creation and the missions of the Word and Spirit. He understands creation as the expression of the divine goodness, the free self-expression of an ecstatic and fecund God. In Bonaventure's wisdom theology, all reality is stamped with the Trinity at every level. The whole world is a symbol of the Trinity. The whole cosmos emanates from its trinitarian exemplar and reflects the trinitarian order at various levels and degrees. It is like a book which reflects its trinitarian author at three levels: at the level of vestige, of image, and of similitude. Every creature is a vestige representing the Trinity in a distant and unclear way. The image, found only in intellectual creatures, reflects the Trinity in a closer and more distinct way. The similitude is that most intense reflection which is found in the rational spirit that is conformed to God through grace.

Bonaventure recognizes that this divine self-expression in creation points to a greater self-expression within the Trinity. In other words, the dynamism, self-expressiveness, and fruitfulness (or fecundity) of the Trinity in creation points to those very realities within the Trinity itself. Bonaventure concludes that in the Trinity there is the procession of the Word in an exemplary manner, by way of nature, from the fecund, ecstatic divine goodness.[66] The principle of exemplarity functions as the second metaphysical principle in Bonaventure's work. (Note that Bonaventure rejects the notion in the trinitarian theologies of Augustine and Aquinas that the Son proceeds by way of intellect.) The procession of the Spirit, on the other hand, is from the divine will, by way of liberality and love. Bonaventure engages the term *circumincessio* (from the root, *circum-in-cedere,* to move around one another), rather than the more sedentary notion of *circuminsessio* (from the Latin root, *circum-in-sedere,* to sit around), to describe the profound and dynamic trinitarian communion of interdependence and mutuality.

Bonaventure then pushes beyond an understanding of the divine nature as the rich fountain from which the entire created universe flows to argue that the concept of primacy may be traced into the very depths of the divine nature itself, as the characteristic of the first divine person. As the divine nature is absolutely prior with respect to all other essences, the Father is the first with respect to the other persons. Hence there is, in God, one in whom resides the fullness of divine fecundity with respect to the divine persons. We must note at this point, however, that Bonaventure's emphasis on the primacy of the First Person is inevitably associated with the dangers of subordination and heirarchy. For this very reason, Edwards gives primacy in his theology to Richard of St. Victor's social model of the Trinity with its stress on mutuality and equality.

For Bonaventure, however, the life of the Trinity originates in the First Person, the Fountain Fullness *(fontalis plenitudo),* who is perfectly expressed in the Second Person, the Word, the eternal Exemplar, and whose mutual love reaches its consummation in the Spirit, who is the love between them. "Word" is Bonaventure's preferred name for the Second Person. It expresses not only the relation of generation between First and Second Persons, but also the relationship of the Son with creation and its salvation. The eternal Exemplar is the self-expression of the trinitarian God and also the Exemplar for every created reality. The eternal Word is the "eternal Art" *(ars aeterna)* of the trinitarian God, from which the truth and beauty of all creation flows. Every creature in its form, proportion, and beauty reflects the Word and Wisdom of God.

Christology and trinitarian theology are inseparably connected in Bonaventure's theology; one approaches the mystery of the Trinity by means of the mystery of Christ. While the Trinity is understood as the exemplar of the world, the mystery of exemplarity is effectively concentrated in the Second Person as the One who is the total expression of all that the divine love is in itself and in relation to the finite. The entire triune structure of God is thus focused in the Word in an exemplary way. In Bonaventure's theology, the role of Exemplar is proper to the Second Person. The Word is the Image of the Fountain Fullness and the divine Exemplar for creation. Following Richard of St. Victor, Bonaventure also understands the Trinity in terms of mutual love. He too explains the procession of the Holy Spirit in terms of *condilectus.*

Edwards finds in Bonaventure's trinitarian theology a rich and dynamic image of the divine reality that is particularly well suited to his theological goal. God is the rich and fecund mystery whose eternal being is a dynamic ecstasy of goodness and love, a dynamic and fecund Trinity of persons. Creation is understood as God's self-expression, the Word as the Exemplar for all things, all creatures existing by way of exemplarity, and as such recognized as inherently revelatory signs of God, as works of art, as kinds of sculpture, representing and expressing the Wisdom of God. From this perspective, the world is recognized as the objectification of the self-knowledge of God, wherein every creature is an aspect of God's self-expression in the world, in its inner structure, reflecting God's dynamic trinitarian presence; as holding the creature in existence (Fountain Fullness), as exemplary cause (Divine Wisdom), and final cause (Spirit of Love). It necessarily follows that the destruction or extinction of various forms of life becomes an issue of properly and profoundly theological concern, for species of life which are being destroyed are modes of God's self-communication and presence.

An Ecological Theology of the Trinitarian God

We can agree with Edwards that Bonaventure's trinitarian theology, in which the world is a vast symbol of the Trinity and the economy is ontologically grounded in the immanent trinitarian mystery of God, offers a remarkably rich and strong basis for an ecological theology that is apt to appeal to contemporary consciousness. Borrowing elements from Richard of St. Victor and Bonaventure, yet careful to avoid the dangers inherent therein, Edwards proposes that we may comprehend the trinitarian relations with creation in terms of both a model of mutual relationships and a model of dynamic and ecstatic self-communication. He proposes the following six theses for an ecological theology of the trinitarian God:[67]

1. The Trinity can be understood as Persons-in-Mutual-Relations, in a communion of love that is radically equal and one; creation can be understood as this Trinity's free, loving relationship with a world of creatures.
2. If the Trinity is understood as Persons-in-Mutual-Love, then relationship, and not simply being or substance, can be understood as the primary metaphysical category. Ultimate reality is understood as Persons-in-Dynamic-Communion.
3. The trinitarian God is a God of dynamic, ecstatic, and fecund self-communication; creation is the free overflow of this divine fecundity, the self-expression of the trinitarian God, so that each creature is a mode and a sign of divine presence.
4. On the basis of the doctrine of the Trinity as Persons-in-Mutual-Communion, human beings can be understood not primarily as isolated individual subjectivities, but as persons-in-relationship, as persons who are both self-possessed and self-giving in communion.
5. Creation is the action of the whole Trinity, but it needs to be seen as involving the distinct roles of the trinitarian Persons, which are not only "appropriated" to them, but "proper" to them.
6. The Trinity's interaction with creation is characterized by the vulnerability and liberating power of love. This trinitarian love respects both the freedom of human beings and the integrity of natural processes.

A theology of the trinitarian God as Persons-in-Mutual-Relationship grounds the distinctly relational understanding of all being that is so prized by the ecological imagination. From a distinctly theological perspective, relationship emerges as the primary ontological category. Theology in this way meets ecology by showing that reality is relational at its most fundamental level, and thereby supporting the relational and communal ecological worldview. The ramifications are significant, as Edwards explains:

> If we view relationships as the primary reality, then this means that we can begin to see all of creation, the universe itself, the biosphere on Earth, individual ecosystems, a living tree, a cell, or a proton, as fundamentally relational and part of a network of interrelationships.[68]

Edwards' accent on relationality as the primary ontological category inevitably raises a challenge to a number of aspects of classical trinitarian theology. He argues, for example, that we need to go beyond the classical understanding to see distinct and proper and not merely appropriated roles in creation, roles that are strictly proper to each Person. The classical theological tradition understands that the works of the Trinity *ad extra,* in other words in the economy of salvation, are one. Creation, for example, is the work of the Trinity as a united and indivisible and, in this particular sense, *undifferentiated* whole, the godhead. The strategy of "appropriation" is then used to reclaim for each of the divine persons a particular role, as appropriate to that divine person, in the divine activity *ad extra.* Edwards, however, presses to an understanding of creation as the work of the united but *differentiated* Trinity, with each Person having a unique role that is strictly proper to that particular Person. Edwards explains:

> The universe, in this view, can be understood as the self-expression of the *trinitarian* God. The Fountain Fullness is the Unoriginate Origin, the Well-Spring and Source of Being for all creatures. Jesus, the divine Wisdom, is the One

in whom all things are created and the One in whom all will
be reconciled. The Holy Spirit is the immanent presence of
God, the Giver of Life, who sustains and renews all things in
the process of continuing creation, and is the Love which
unites all creatures and will bring all to completion.[69]

Edwards also proposes, again contrary to classical understanding, that God has a real and not just a logical relation with
the world, and that God freely accepts the limitations and vulnerability of such a relationship. In other words, Edwards would persuade us that God allows and respects not only human freedom
but also the freedom of natural processes. He argues that we can
understand that God freely creates in such a way as to be commit-
ted to the integrity of all the processes of the universe. In this way,
we can also understand that there are limits to the divine power,
limits set by love and respect for creation. Edward's theology thus
suggests

a vision of the trinitarian God engaged in ongoing creation
in the way that is consonant with radical love—not out of a
static predetermined plan, but responsively, adventurously
and inventively...God's artistry is freely limited by God's
loving respect for the dynamics of an emergent universe.
But within the limitations set by love and respect for creation, the divine artistry is endlessly creative.[70]

Edwards argues that two fundamental principles follow from
this trinitarian theology for an expressly ecological theology:[71]

1. The trinitarian God is to be understood as Persons-in-Mutual-
    Communion. Relationships of mutual love undergird the
    expanding universe and hold all things together. The God of
    mutual relations freely and reciprocally interrelates with all
    creatures in ways which respect their identity. Reality is fun-
    damentally interrelationship, and human beings are called to
    see themselves as in some way kin with all other creatures.
2. The trinitarian God is a God of dynamic and fecund self-

expression. Every species and every creature is God's self-expression, a word of God, a sign of the trinitarian God, a mode of divine presence.

In this theological imagining, all creation is understood in terms of the trinitarian God who created it. Salvation emerges as a concept that embraces the whole of creation, involving a transformation of the whole universe. Furthermore, in this thoroughly theocentric view, the fruit of a Wisdom Christology and a trinitarian theology in the tradition of Bonaventure, whereby each creature is the free act of divine self-expression, things have value in *themselves* because each is the self-expression, symbol, and sacrament of the triune God. Each is the created articulation of the eternal Word, the divine Wisdom, the Art of God. As Edwards explains:

> This means that the rain forest of the Amazon is to be understood as the self-expression of the divine Trinity. It is a sacrament of God's presence. Its vitality and exuberance spring from the immanent presence of the Spirit, the giver of life. They express the trinitarian love of life. The rain forest, in its form, function and beauty as a harmonious biotic community is the work of art of divine Wisdom. The species of plants and animals which are being destroyed forever are modes of God's self-communication and presence.[77]

A theology of the intrinsic value of all creatures, together with a respect for the unique dignity of the human person, clearly emerges.[73] Moreover, when God is understood in terms of Persons-in-Mutual-Relationship and the divine dynamic and ecstatic fecundity, the very *diversity* of living creatures itself emerges as the self-expression of divine fruitfulness. We arrive at the point of profound respect and reverence not just for life or for individual animals or plants but for the diversity of living systems and interacting ecosystems.

A theological anthropology follows, whereby: (1) the human person is profoundly and intrinsically interconnected with every other creature, participating in a community of persons-in-mutual relationship in the whole community of creatures; and (2) the human person has the particular dignity and responsibility which comes from being one in whom the universe has come to self-awareness.[74] In this way, Edwards finally arrives at an ecological praxis, on the basis of an understanding of human beings as self-conscious creatures invited into conscious interpersonal relationships with the Creator and to partnership with the Creator in care for creation.

In this brief survey of Edwards' thought, we see how he moves from the Wisdom tradition of the scriptures to a Wisdom Christology, from thence to a "wisdom ecology" or an ecological theology with tangible ethical ramifications. In Edwards' theology, a theology of Jesus as the divine Wisdom firmly grounds both a Christian approach to ecology and an ecological understanding of the triune God. What is remarkable is that his integration of Christian theology, ecology, and praxis is firmly grounded in an understanding of the trinitarian God of mutual love and fecundity. Edwards makes a valuable contribution not only to ecological theology but to contemporary trinitarian theology, manifestly meeting the cosmic scope of the present challenge to the theological imagination.

5
The Trinity and Jesus' Paschal Mystery—Hans Urs von Balthasar

The three trinitarian theologies which we have so far considered look to find the relevance and ramifications of our belief in the doctrine of the Trinity for Christian praxis. Swiss theologian Hans Urs von Balthasar takes an entirely different approach. He is concerned that classical Augustinian-Thomistic trinitarian theology simply does not convey the mystery of the Trinity in terms of its intensely dramatic engagement with us in the world of suffering, and in the sheer splendor of divine love that is revealed to us in the person of Jesus. He believes that a much fuller and richer explication of the mystery is both possible and necessary. His explication of the mystery of the Trinity, through its interconnection with the paschal mystery of Jesus' death and resurrection, is firmly rooted in the events of the salvation history and, in fact, right at the point of the Trinity's engagement with us in our greatest darkness, death itself. Salvation must surely touch the human person here of all places, when the human person is at "wit's end,"—in most dire need.

While standing firmly within the Roman Catholic tradition, von Balthasar is averse to adopting a philosophical system and then applying it to the biblical data, in the way of Aquinas's approach. He returns to the biblical narrative with the express intention to give primacy to the data of God's self-revelation. He also recognizes that the intrinsically dynamic character of the divine being, traditionally expressed in terms of processions, relations, and missions, has been seriously weakened in traditional Latin trinitarian theology, which fails to convey the sheer liveliness and vitality of the divine interpersonal relations to which the events of salvation history so strongly attest. A tendency to essentialism in the tradition, a focus on the essence (the "what is") of persons and things as distinct from their more existentialist or personalist meaning, has obscured the dynamism inherent in Aquinas's description of God as Pure Act, *Actus Purus.*

It is the dynamism and the sheer glory of the divine love which von Balthasar sees as having been overlooked by so much of the Latin theological tradition and which he strives to render more fully. He writes: "God's message to man in Christ…is credible only as love—and here we mean God's own love, the manifestation of which is the manifestation of the glory of God."[75] Here is von Balthasar's *leitmotif:* love alone is credible. Love alone is credible, he explains, because it is the only thing which is truly intelligible, truly "rational." Only love makes sense of it all. It is the sheer glory of God's love, revealed most dramatically in Jesus' descent into hell, which lies at the heart of his theology. He wants us to behold the sheer glory of God, and in beholding, to believe and to adore.

Von Balthasar is emphatic in rejecting the classical psychological analogy as an adequate elucidation of the mystery. He insists that the immanent processions be understood not as the processions of intellect and will but as processions of love. It is a procession of love which issues in the Son, who enters into creation, and descends into the depths of hell for us and for our salvation. It is also a procession of love that issues in the person of the Holy Spirit, spirit of the love of Father and Son. Both processions are processions of love. In this way, von Balthasar effectively proposes a newly fashioned trinitarian ontology, in which love, and the relationality of love, as distinct from an ontology of substance, has primacy in explicating the mystery.

What is remarkable is that, for von Balthasar, the doctrine of Trinity has its center and origin in the events of those three days of the *Sacrum Triduum,* with the descent into hell on Holy Saturday as its midpoint. He writes, "For it is precisely in the Kenosis of Christ (and nowhere else) that the *inner* majesty of God's love appears, of God who 'is love' (1 John 4:8) and therefore a trinity."[76] In Jesus' paschal mystery, von Balthasar recognizes that God has not just redeemed the world but disclosed God's own being.[77] We see in "the Lord's actions...not only a sublime *metaphor* of eternal love, but Eternal Love itself."[78]

The Innertrinitarian "Event"

Central to von Balthasar's theology of the paschal mystery and its interconnection with the Trinity is the insight that the trinitarian processions, as traditionally understood, already imply movement and dynamism in God. Von Balthasar argues that the very grounds for the possibility in the economy of the incarnation and the paschal mystery are to be found in "what one can, by analogy, designate as the eternal 'event' of the divine processions."[79] He explains:

> That God (as Father) can so give away his divinity that God (as Son) does not merely receive it as something borrowed, but possesses it in the equality of essence, expresses such an unimaginable and unsurpassable "separation" of God from Godself that every other separation (made possible by it!), even the most dark and bitter, can only occur within this first separation.[80]

In other words, the separation and union of the paschal event are grounded in the separation and union within the eternal innertrinitarian "event" of divine life. In that "event," in this drama which is constitutive of the triune God, the Father does not cling to his divinity, but "in an eternal 'super-Kenosis,' makes himself 'destitute' of all that he is and can be so as to bring forth a consubstantial divinity, the Son."[81] Von Balthasar recognizes that here, in this primordial "separation" of God from God lies, from all eternity, the "space" for all the contingencies of human freedom. He understands that every possible drama between God and the world is in this way already contained in, allowed for, and indeed infinitely surpassed and transcended in that eternal, supra-temporal "event" of innertrinitarian love, wherein the Father begets the Son. As von Balthasar explains: "It is a case of the play within the play: our play 'plays' in his play."[82] The drama between God and the world lies within this primordial innertrinitarian "drama" between God and God.

> We are saying that the "emptying" of the Father's heart in the begetting of the Son includes and surpasses every possible drama between God and the world, because a world can only have its place within the difference between the Father and the Son which is held open and bridged over by the Spirit.[83]

The whole salvation event is thus understood to occur within the eternal divine event whereby the Father generates the Son. In more technical terms, the innertrinitarian "event" of self-giving and self-emptying love is the condition of the possibility of divine activity in kenotic events *ad extra,* containing within itself all the modalities of love, such as kenosis, abandonment, suffering, death, and descent, which appear in creation in the course of salvation history. This means that the kenotic form of Jesus Christ in the paschal mystery is not new or foreign to God, but is, in fact, thoroughly consistent with this eternal supra-temporal "event" of triune love. It is, in fact, the created form, the revelation, of what is always already in God. In von Balthasar's theology, all forms of kenosis *ad extra* are contained within this primal kenosis *ad intra,* whereby the Father begets the Son. The

Father's generation of the Son represents the first kenosis and underpins all other forms of kenosis. It manifests the utter self-giving of the Father to the Son, a self-yielding surrender of divine being. The Son's self-giving to the Father in his death on a cross is already contained within this eternal procession: in fact, it is a modality of the Son's procession.

In this way, von Balthasar uses the term "event," qualified by the use of "supra-temporal," to convey a liveliness and vitality within God, which is inherent in that difference-in-unity at the heart of the classical trinitarian theology, but which traditional notions of immutability and impassibility fail to communicate.

Von Balthasar assiduously avoids any univocal attribution of mutability or passibility to God. God does not become what God was not. However, von Balthasar does mean that strict notions of immutability and impassibility are not theologically tenable. In the brilliant light of the revelation of God in Jesus' paschal mystery, von Balthasar posits a real kenosis in God which is not merely functional but ontological. The notion of the innertrinitarian "event" of triune love thus leads von Balthasar to modify substantially the traditional understanding of the divine attributes and to attribute receptivity, "supra-kenosis," "supra-mutability," increase and even "suffering" to God, as divine perfections. Process notions are, nonetheless, explicitly rejected: God does not need the world and its processes in order to become Godself. This notion of "event" is always used by von Balthasar to describe a liveliness in God which is "supra-temporal."

The Trinity and the Paschal Mystery

The Cross

For von Balthasar, the cross, and indeed the whole paschal mystery, is an event of triune surrender, of mutual self-giving and self-yielding love. It is revelation of this innertrinitarian reality. The separation to the point of the Father's abandonment of the

Son to death on the cross is a modality of the innertrinitarian "event." The cross reveals that it is of the Son's very being to hold nothing for himself but to yield everything to the Father. His obedience is constitutive of his identity as the Son, expressive of his divine sonship and freedom. Furthermore, this obedience is not a form of subservience or subordination of the Son in relation to the Father but is, instead, an expression of his sovereign liberty as the divine Son. Von Balthasar explains:

> The obedience with which the Son performs the Father's will is not the obedience of a "serf"…it quite evidently comes from God himself; it is the freedom which reigns between Father and Son.[84]

Here too von Balthasar recognizes that Jesus' obedience is the translation or expression, in the economy, of the Son's innertrinitarian love for the Father: "…his obedience presents the kenotic translation of the eternal love of the Son for the 'ever greater' Father."[85] Its archetype is the filial love of the Son for the Father in the Trinity *ad intra,* his receptivity and responsiveness to the Father and all that the Father has to give him.

Von Balthasar also recognizes that Jesus' mission in the economy is most profoundly and solely appropriate to his divine person. The mission of Jesus, which he fulfills by his obedience, is uniquely and properly his own, an expression of his person as the Son. Aquinas's notion that any of the Three could have become incarnate and accomplished the redemptive mission is quite alien to von Balthasar's understanding.[86] In fact, von Balthasar's concept of person, whether human or divine, is rooted in the concept of mission *(Sendung).* As he explains:

> It is when God addresses a conscious subject, tells him who he is and what he means to the eternal God of truth and shows him the purpose of his existence—that is, imparts a distinctive and divinely authorized mission—that we can say of a conscious subject that he is a "person."[87]

Von Balthasar argues that a *Geistessubjekt* (a conscious subject) has intellect and will, but becomes a *person* in the mission which he or she receives from God. Here again, in distinguishing between a *Geistessubjekt* and a person, von Balthasar effectively rejects the classical treatment of the processions by way of the psychological analogy.

Descent into Hell

Von Balthasar's treatment of the descent into hell is one of the most striking features of his whole theology. The portrayal of the descent into hell is like the magnificent centerpiece of the breathtaking triptych that is von Balthasar's trinitarian theology. It is also highly controversial, for there is little direct biblical warrant for his extraordinary emphasis on this aspect of the paschal mystery. In this emphasis on the descent, he is profoundly inspired by the mystical experiences and visionary theology of Adrienne von Speyr, whose mystical experience of Christ's descent into hell was a central insight.[88] Under her influence, von Balthasar makes the extraordinary claim that Holy Saturday stands in "the mysterious middle between cross and resurrection, and consequently properly in the center of all revelation and theology."[89]

Far from being an active descent, von Balthasar understands the descent as an utterly passive "sinking down." First, and most obviously, it reveals Jesus' solidarity in human death. However, the descent also represents Jesus' solidarity with humanity in its sinfulness. In the descent, Jesus, in the utter defenselessness of love, enters into the loneliness and desolation of the sinner.

> Into this finality (of death) the dead Son descends, no longer acting in any way, but stripped by the cross of every power and initiative of his own as one purely to be used, debased to mere matter, with a fully indifferent (corpse) obedience, incapable of any active solidarity. Only thus is he right for

any "sermon" to the dead. He is (out of ultimate love however) dead together with them. And exactly in that way he disturbs the absolute loneliness striven for by the sinner: the sinner, who wants to be "damned" apart from God, finds God again in his loneliness, but God in the absolute weakness of love who unfathomably in the period of nontime enters into solidarity with those damning themselves.[90]

Von Balthasar's treatment of the descent into hell allows him to explore the hoary question of the relationship between divine and created freedom. In von Balthasar's theology of the paschal mystery, the divine persons are in fact revealed precisely in their dramatic engagement with the reality of human freedom. The descent shows that God, by accompanying the sinner in hell, freely and lovingly shares in the exercise of human freedom. The reality of human freedom, including the dramatic possibility of rejecting God, is radically affirmed and respected. Only in the absolute weakness and vulnerability of love does God descend into hell to accompany the sinner in his or her choice. Notwithstanding, God's freedom is not thwarted by created human freedom, as von Balthasar explains:

One would still be able to say that God gives human beings the capacity to perform what seems for human beings to be a definitive (negative) choice against God, but which does not need to be judged/evaluated/assessed by God as definitive. And not in such a way that the human person's choice is called into question from outside—which would amount to a disregard of the freedom bestowed on it—but rather in such a way that God with his own divine choice, accompanies the human person into the most extreme situation of his (negative) choice. This is what happens in the passion of Jesus.[91]

In von Balthasar's theology of the descent, even hell is understood as a "sphere" in God. Hell remains as a real possibility of genuine human freedom, but it is gathered up into the Trinity, to exist in the boundless creativity and compassion of the

Trinity's all-embracing love. Even the chaos of sin is allowed for and mysteriously accommodated in the innertrinitarian "event." Von Balthasar explains:

> Creaturely freedom and its future can only be gathered up into the sphere of God without loss and prejudice if they are allowed their full range of open possibilities within the sphere of the world and if this sphere is nevertheless under stood as a sphere *in God*, which God can enter, can determine, in which he can work his purposes. He does enter it, determine it, achieve his purposes in it in the death, descent into hell, and resurrection of the Son of God;... But it is all-embracing not as a boundary imposed upon it from without but as an opening up from within, as God shares in the exercise of human freedom, of new horizons which outstrip the possibilities of such freedom.[92]

The trinitarian character of the descent is crucial to von Balthasar's theology, for the descent is in fact only possible because God is triune. The Father sends the Son into hell. The Son, *while remaining God,* descends into God-forsakenness, to assume the condition of sinful humanity. As the God-forsaken Son of God and, in this sense, as one who is even more lonely,[93] Jesus accompanies the sinner who has chosen to damn himself or herself and to reject God. Throughout, he remains God. The Spirit accompanies him and is the bond between Father and Son, uniting them in their separation. The abandonment of the Son by the Father is possible only because, at this point of extreme separation, they are united in love by the Holy Spirit:

> This opposition between God, the creative origin (the "Father"), and the man who, faithful to the mission of the origin, ventures on into the ultimate perdition (the "Son"), this bond stretched to breaking point does not break because the same Spirit of absolute love (the "Spirit") informs both the one who sends and the one sent. God causes God to go

into abandonment by God, while accompanying him on the way with his Spirit.[94]

For von Balthasar, it is precisely and preeminently in the descent into hell that the glory of the Lord is revealed:

> It is "glory" in the uttermost opposite of "glory," because it is at the same time blind obedience that must obey the Father at the point where the last trace of God seems lost (in pure sin), together with every other communication (in pure solitariness).[95]

It is absolute glory because it is absolute love; it is love even when rejected. This is the essential meaning and significance of the descent. Here again, "love alone is credible." In the descent God, who is love, freely takes responsibility for the success of creation, in the context of human freedom and sin. Love enters into the realm of death and desolation, gathering our lostness into God's triune self, revealing the sheer graciousness, boundless compassion, and utter glory of the love that is God. The descent into hell means that no place is cut off from the love of God. Even hell belongs to Christ; even hell is mysteriously taken up and into the trinitarian communion of love, ever allowed for in the primordial event of trinitarian love. It means that nobody is God-forsaken, not even the person who chooses to reject God's love. It means that the last word is not suffering or death or desolation or lostness: the last word, the ever-present and undying word, is love.

The Resurrection

It is only with the resurrection that we perceive fully the trinitarian character of the paschal events. In the resurrection the revelation of the Trinity appears in clear light—the Father to whom is attributed the initiative in raising the Son, the Son who appears as the Living One, and the Spirit who is sent forth into the world.[96] While the Father takes the initiative in raising the Son and, as Creator, brings his salvific plan for creation to its completion in the resurrection, the resurrection of Jesus is actually accomplished in the powerful transfiguring action of the Spirit of God.[97] The Holy Spirit is also the "instrument" and "milieu" of the resurrection.[98] It was the Spirit who "held open and bridged over" the separation of the Father and the Son in the cross and descent into hell.[99]

In Jesus' life out of death, the wounds of his self-surrendering love remain. He is the Slain Lamb. This image of the Slain Lamb is another powerful and pervasive one in von Balthasar's theology; it is effectively emblematic of his vision of the trinitarian relations as relations of total self-surrender in love, as revealed in the paschal mystery. As von Balthasar explains:

> This new life that has definitively put death behind itself (Rom 6:10) remains nevertheless life out of death, life characterized by its passage through death. It is life which on the one hand has power over death...but on the other hand remains profoundly marked by the event and experience of death insofar as this highest achievement of life was—and remains—the same as total self-surrender.[100]

Von Balthasar perceives that the paschal mystery itself, the "inseparable unity" of death and resurrection, is iconically expressed in the very body of the Risen Lord, risen in its woundedness. Once again, we see how incarnationally concrete von Balthasar's theology is.

The Divine Perfections

Von Balthasar's theology explores the mystery of the Trinity by connecting it to Jesus' paschal mystery and the mystery of love which it reveals. A distinct shift in emphasis from "being" to "love" results, a shift that is grounded in the insight that God is revealed in the paschal mystery, not as the fullness of being, but as the sheer glory of love. Hence God's being and the trinitarian processions are presented, not in terms of metaphysically-conceived absolute being, *Actus Purus, Ipsum Esse,* but rather in terms of the intrinsically dynamic *Actus Purus, Ipsum Amare.* Von Balthasar does not, however, deny the validity of the traditional substance-based metaphysics. Neither does he step outside of traditional notions of processions in God. Technically speaking, his notion of the innertrinitarian "event" is thoroughly consistent with and actually implicit in the traditional understanding of divine processions, even if not previously elaborated in this way.

Von Balthasar's very daring way of speaking of the trinitarian love, together with a very untraditional stress on the receptivity of love and the boundless variety of modalities that love can assume, leads to a very new understanding of the divine attributes. In terms of immutability and impassibility, again he does not repudiate the patristic and scholastic tradition.[101] Nevertheless, he does consider that a fuller understanding is possible, one that more adequately expresses the trinitarian dynamism which the paschal mystery so clearly discloses. The paschal mystery reveals that God is manifestly more glorious than philosophically fashioned notions of immutability and impassibility could either convey or admit. Note, however, that von Balthasar makes no univocal attribution of change, temporality, or suffering to God: something analogous, but *only* analogous, to such notions as these can be understood as divine perfections. Nor does God become what God was not: God is, in the paschal mystery, what God eternally is.

In this way, in stark contrast to the traditional Thomistic approach to trinitarian theology which had its understanding of the processions mediated through the metaphysically fashioned psychological analogy, von Balthasar focuses on Jesus in his paschal mystery and constructs his trinitarian theology on the basis of the trinitarian relationality which is revealed there. Instead of a rather abstract and ahistorical inquiry, which privileges the psychological analogy rather than the biblical data, the mystery of the Trinity is approached as the mystery of this three-personed God who has saved us, gathering our lostness into God's triune life of love. At the very least, von Balthasar issues a powerful challenge to the hegemony which the psychological analogy has enjoyed in traditional Latin trinitarian theology for centuries. But the remarkable novelty of his trinitarian theology lies in the recognition that the paschal mystery is not only redemptive but revelatory. Admittedly, the traditional approach accords a redemptive meaning to the death and resurrection of Jesus. But von Balthasar recognizes the paschal mystery as having properly theological meaning. It sheds light on the divine being itself, revealing God's inner triune relationships. In other words, von Balthasar perceives that Jesus' paschal mystery is revelatory of God's mode of acting and God's mode of being, and that this is so not just in relation to us and our salvation, but as it is in itself in eternity. Where Boff, Johnson, and Edwards have explored various kinds of social models for the Trinity and their implications for human life and community, von Balthasar would instead have us understand that the paschal mystery is analogy, properly speaking, of trinitarian life.

From this perspective, depicted so dramatically by von Balthasar, we begin to perceive that it is no accident that the revelation of the mystery of the Trinity takes place in the dynamic modality of Jesus' paschal mystery. We glimpse, as if through a dark glass but dimly, that it is intrinsically appropriate to the divine being to express itself in precisely this way. In this resides von Balthasar's profound insight, and in this consists his bracing challenge to trinitarian theology: that the paschal movement somehow conveys, like an icon, the eternal trinitarian relations in a paradigmatic way which is, of its very essence, expressive of the eternal trinitarian relationality.

6
Trinity of Love:
The Psychological Analogy Revisited

In our previous explorations of newly-emerging forms of trinitarian theology, we have seen that the authors whose works we have examined effectively set aside the traditional Latin form of explication of trinitarian theology. Classical trinitarian theology would seem to be so abstract and remote from our experience as to be practically irrelevant. Yet the traditional Latin treatment of the mystery of the Trinity, which reaches its apogee in Aquinas's explication, is unarguably an unparalleled feat of logic, coherence, and systematic exposition. The psychological analogy has enjoyed an esteemed status as a most plausible and persuasive explanation of the processions which constitute the triune godhead for almost two millennia since first proposed by Augustine, then elegantly expressed in refined metaphysical terms by Aquinas, reaffirmed in the catechism of the Council of Trent and in numerous papal documents, and well entrenched as common doctrine until relatively recently. But clearly, logic, coherence, and systematic exposition do not suffice to render theology meaningful. The classical form of trinitarian theology is evidently neither disclosive nor persuasive in the contemporary context, as is clearly evident in a variety of alternative approaches we have outlined.

The dissatisfaction with the classical form of trinitarian theology goes much deeper than merely functional questions concerning the *ordo doctrinae* or the apparent abstraction and remoteness of the traditional explication from the biblical data. We live in a very different world and a very different cultural milieu than the medievals. Today even the question of the existence of God has become culturally problematic. This change in cultural milieu and the emergence in modern consciousness of new exigences inevitably and profoundly affects the theological enterprise, demanding new forms of mediation of meaning. It is this change which has rendered the classical mediation of the mystery obsolete. As acknowledged by Vatican II, "the human race has passed from a static concept of reality to a more dynamic, evolutionary one. In consequence, there has arisen a new series of problems, a series as important as can be, calling for new efforts of analysis and synthesis."[102] Hence, for example, the emergence and the appeal of process theology in contemporary theological thinking. After all, the process model concurs with so much of our experience and understanding of the universe and the dynamic interrelatedness of reality. Its understanding of God as compassionately involved in the emerging processive cosmos, as affected by our history, offers an apparently more comprehensible response to the problem of evil. The problem, however, is that the process system of thought tends to reduce an explication of the divine mystery into terms of just the one concept: process. Process, rather than God, then constitutes the ultimate.[103]

But the question for us here is whether the classical form of trinitarian theology, and the psychological analogy it engages, is irredeemably obsolete and so hopelessly beyond retrieval as to be set aside once and for all. Surely the favor and status which it has enjoyed in trinitarian theology and the centuries of meaningfulness and persuasive power it has rendered would caution us against too hasty a dismissal. Might it not be the case that the psychological analogy in fact expresses a profound truth about human and divine subjectivity which its medieval metaphysical wrappings obscure from us? The question begs very careful consideration. To use another metaphor, let us take care that we do not throw out the baby with the bathwater!

Australian Redemptorist theologian Anthony (Tony) Kelly addresses precisely this question. He adopts a very different approach compared to our other authors. He comes to the question with a refined methodological awareness and recognizes the urgent need for a new form of mediation of the mystery and a new grounding of the psychological analogy. However, he does not abandon traditional trinitarian theology, but instead seeks to reclaim it by refashioning it in a way that is more apt to appeal to contemporary consciousness.[104] He is acutely aware that if trinitarian theology is to mediate meaning it must be a source of transformative meaning in human affairs and exercise a redemptive influence in the context of our contemporary struggle with evil in all its dehumanizing forms. Consequently, he is not slow to apply trinitarian meaning to the worlds of social action, psychological liberation, ecology, cosmic emergence, interfaith dialogue, and even to feminist concerns. He recognizes that only such a kind of trinitarian theology is in fact genuinely faithful to the Christian realism which prompted the development of the doctrinal forms that are our theological inheritance. But, for Kelly, unlike our other authors, the challenge is that of a critical retrieval of the classical psychological analogy.

A Critical Retrieval of the Classical Psychological Analogy

Kelly situates an exploration of the history and development of trinitarian theology and then his own development of the meaning of the mystery of the Trinity in terms of the three classical techniques of theological reflection, as described by Vatican I: analogy, interconnection, and eschatological liberation.

> If human reason, with faith as its guiding light, enquires earnestly, devoutly, and circumspectly, it does reach, by God's generosity, some understanding of the mysteries, and

that a most profitable one. It does this by analogy with the truths it knows naturally, and also from the interconnection of the mysteries with one another, and in reference to the final end of man.[105]

The tradition of trinitarian theology which culminates in Thomas Aquinas's synthesis relies principally on the technique of analogy. Aquinas's synthesis is undoubtedly an elegant and metaphysically austere exercise in analogical thinking that is productive of a striking systematic coherence. Nonetheless, as Kelly explains, its meaningfulness and usefulness depends on a metaphysics of being, soul, and faculties which is frankly no longer accepted or understood. The Thomistic mediation of meaning has consequently broken down in the contemporary context. Divorced from the metaphysical framework which supports it, it is simply unable to function effectively in mediating religious meaning. Furthermore, from the perspective of modern empirically organized culture, not only is the metaphysically fashioned psychological analogy remote from the contemporary experience of self, the Thomistic explication of trinitarian theology also seems very far removed from the biblical data concerning the actual events of salvation history. Kelly recognizes that, if the classical doctrine is to be persuasive and disclosive in contemporary culture, it clearly needs to be transposed into more experiential and existentially meaningful terms.

Inspired by the Johannine confession that "God is Love," Kelly therefore proposes a transposition from the medieval metaphysically fashioned doctrinal system of Thomas Aquinas. Kelly intends a more phenomenologically based account of religious and Christian experience. To this end, he addresses scripturally given psychological data in a new way: the experience of life as originally, radically, and ultimately Love and the historical experience of Christian faith, whereby the mystery of Love is named and invoked in trinitarian terms. He explains: "That, it seems to me, is the fundamental meaning of the Trinity. There was never a time when God is not Love."[106] In this context, the Father is the Originating Lover; the Son is the self-expression of that Love; and the Spirit is the original and inexhaustible activity of this Love, drawing the created universe into itself.

Kelly proceeds to transpose the Thomistic notion of God as sheer unlimited divine Be-ing, as pure act *(Ipsum Esse Subsistens, Actus Purus)*, to the biblically grounded notion of God as Agape, Love, incarnate in Christ and communicated in the Spirit.[107] In Kelly's theology, the divine reality is explicated in terms of sheer Being-in-Love, constituted as such by being Father, Son and Spirit, three subjects in one conscious infinite act of Being-in-Love. In this way, Kelly effects a transposition from the scholastic metaphysically fashioned psychological analogy to a more phenomenologically oriented description of the mystery, based on the experience of Love that is the very foundation of faith's realism. The philosophical account of the psychological analogy thus gives way to a psychological account of faith's experience. The psychological image is regrounded in the paradigmatic Christian experience of God as Love. Relocating the psychological analogy in this fashion, Kelly deftly achieves a passage from classical doctrines to a phenomenology of the Christian experience of communion and, secondly, from the metaphysical mode of analysis to a more experientially and scripturally grounded reflection that is more likely to mediate meaning to contemporary consciousness. There is no denial of the necessity of metaphysics, but rather a recognition of the need for a more appropriate metaphysics to protect the realism of Christian faith in this new context.[108]

Bernard Lonergan's Intentionality Analysis of Human Subjectivity as Experiential Foundation for the Psychological Analogy

From a methodological perspective, Kelly carries forward Bernard Lonergan's effort, in *De Deo Trino,*[109] to transpose the

Augustinian-Thomistic mode of analogical reflection into a contemporary methodological context. In this new context, meaning is no longer elaborated in terms of metaphysical theory, but is grounded in the experience of the existential subject. Lonergan's intentionality analysis of the self-transcending character of human subjectivity provides the framework for Kelly's transposition of the metaphysically elaborated psychological analogy into contemporary experiential terms.[110]

Lonergan's intentionality analysis is based on an investigation of our experience as acting, conscious, intentional human subjects—most radically, our experience of human loving. It does not start with theory or metaphysical principles ("from the outside in," as it were) but with the experience of the concrete, conscious, dynamically acting human subject ("from the inside out"). In other words, it begins from reflection on our selves-in-action, in the movement of self-transcendence that is actualized in our experience, our thoughts, our judgments, our decisions, and our commitments. It attempts to articulate the dynamics of our self-transcending subjectivity—the unfolding dynamics of self-transcendence of the conscious human subject—that is manifest in our attentive, intelligent, responsible, loving selves. In contrast to the classical tradition, which treated the human being as a metaphysical substance distinguished from other natural beings by psychological attributes and powers, intentionality analysis attends to human beings as psychological subjects, conscious persons, intentional subjectivities. By grounding theological terms in intentional subjectivity, we therefore speak in a fundamentally critical way "from experience," to mean reality "from the inside out," as it were, as conscious subjects of experience.

An analysis of our intentional and conscious acts reveals our self-transcending activity. It leads to the realization that human consciousness expands through its interrelated levels of activity, from the empirical level (sensations and consciousness), to the intellectual (acts of understanding), to the rational (acts of judgment), and ultimately to the responsible (decision-making) and the religious (questions and answers about ultimate meaning and value). Intentionality analysis thus brings to light a structure in our experiencing, understanding, judging, and deciding, with each level presupposed, complemented, and sublated by the higher.[111] Our conscious activity is clearly organized around the concerns of disciplined attention, intelligent inquiry, reasonable judgment, and continuing responsibility. These then are the transcendental notions which, according to Lonergan, together constitute the dynamism of conscious intentionality of the human subject. Most pertinent to our concerns here, however, is that, in terms of Lonergan's intentionality analysis, the fulfillment of human existence is a kind of transcendent being-in-love, ultimately a being-in-love with God:

> The transcendental notions, that is, our questions for intelligence, for reflection, for deliberation, constitute our capacity for self-transcendence. This capacity becomes an actuality when one falls in love. Then one's being becomes being-in-love. Such being-in-love has its antecedents, its causes, its conditions, its occasions. But once it has blossomed forth, and as long as it lasts, it takes over. It is the first principle. From it flows one's desires and fears, one's joys and sorrows, one's discernment of values, one's decisions and deeds....As the question of God is implicit in all our questioning, so being in love with God is the basic fulfillment of our conscious intentionality.[112]

Kelly's Correlation: Divine Being-in-Love and Human Being-in-Love

Kelly recognizes that a correlation thus suggests itself—between the foundational Christian experience of God as Love, as Being-in-Love, and human being-in-love—a correlation between the divine self-communication and the unfolding dynamics of our human self-transcendence. Here Kelly finds the key to the transposition he seeks to achieve. The human experience of self-transcending subjectivity, with its peak state of being-in-love, becomes the analogy for the divine Being-in-Love and thus for an understanding of the triune God.

This analogy, when applied to an understanding of God as unrestricted pure Being-in-Love, the *actus purus* of Loving, *Ipsum Amare Subsistens,* yields a plausible explication of the immanent trinitarian processions. In terms of intentionality, we can understand that in God, as infinite self-realization in Love, loving and self transcendence are perfectly identified. The divine Being-in-Love is fully conscious and manifests itself in a judgment grounded on the divine evidence of the infinite value of the divine Love (the Son), and proceeds from that into all the activity of loving (the Spirit). These "processions" ground the relationships within the three-fold subjectivity of the divine Being-in-Love, the Father as originating love, the Son as judgment of value expressing that love, and the Spirit as originated loving. The result of this transposition of the psychological analogy is that the Trinity is a way of expressing God as Love, as self-giving Lovingness. The processions of the Word and Spirit, in the one dynamism of infinite Love, enact the meaning of God as Being-in-Love in the essential self-constitution of the divine being. God is Love, as Love expressed in the Son, and given as Lovable and enabling Loving in the Spirit. Thus, Kelly is able to expound the divine mystery of the Trinity in terms of an eternally self-constituting activity of Being-in-Love, one divine consciousness, articulated in a trinitarian communion of Father, Son, and Spirit. He describes the result as a "procession theology," in contrast to a "process theology" and its inherent limitations.[113]

The divine mystery is constituted as Being-in-Love by being Father, Son, and Spirit: God is originatively Love as Father, expressively Love as Son, communicatively Love as Spirit, three subjects in the one conscious infinite act of Being-in-Love. Each divine person has a distinct and unique meaning in the self-constitution of divine mystery; each is Love in a distinctive manner that is properly its own. The three are intelligible as Trinity only insofar as they manifest the divine mystery as sheer Being-in-Love. The divine *self-giving* as Love is the outcome of the divine *self-possession* as Love. The Love that is given from God, of God, and as God is invoked as Father, Son, and Spirit.

Similarly, love is the context of the language of "Three Persons" in Kelly's trinitarian theology.[114] Theologically speaking, the notion of person serves to express the experience of the three-fold self-differentiated reality of God as Love (Lover, the truth of Love, and the gift of Love). The use of the language of "persons" serves to clarify the meaning of the biblical experience of God as triune and effectively secures the realism of God's invocability as Father, Son, and Spirit. It enables us to express the intensely personal trinitarian reality as differentiated into three distinct subjects, interrelated in the one divine consciousness of Being-in-Love. Kelly sees no need to qualify the usefulness of the terminology of "person" in trinitarian theology, despite difficulties inherent in the modern psychological notion of person as an individual center of consciousness. To the contrary, Kelly would persuade us that the use of the language of "person" is a salutary reminder that theology is exploring a mystery of Love.

The communion with Father, Son, and Spirit which believers enjoy, the divine indwelling which they experience, is an entry into the divine consciousness of Being-in-Love. Moreover, Christian faith discerns that the divine Being-in-Love, Father, Son, and Spirit, is communicated to global and not merely individual experience. A globally oriented Christian faith, a new global consciousness, a global being-in-love, emerges. Hence, in Kelly's hands, the psychological analogy of the Trinity works in two directions. First, it provides terms for exploring the trinitarian consciousness of being-in-love. Second, it points to the manner in which divine love communicates itself to the mind and heart and creativity of human consciousness within a cultural and global context.

The cross reveals that the divine self-transcending Love is manifest as self-sacrifice. "Thus, to a world afflicted by the excess of the problem of evil, the Trinity communicates itself in another excess: that of a Mystery of self-giving Love."[115] The cross reveals a certain undeniable quality of refusal: this divine Being-in-Love refuses to be anything other than itself. Here the Trinity is revealed as the Love that keeps on being Love in a way that overcomes the power of death. This Being-in-Love comes to its own victory in the resurrection of the Crucified, and in the history of self-sacrificing love it energizes. While the cross reveals the unconditional character of the love at work, the resurrection of the Crucified points to the transformation of the universe that has begun.

The whole universe is drawn into the realm of the divine through the incarnation, cross, and resurrection of the Son and through the sending of the Spirit. Though the missions are projections of the divine reality into creation, as traditionally understood, the transcendent purpose of such "sendings" is that finite reality might come to exist in God in a radically new way. In this sense, Son and Spirit are sent for the sake of enfolding all in God, in the one realm of Being-in-Love. Reflection on this understanding of the Word incarnated, the Spirit infused, and the Father intimated leads Kelly to the more cosmic configuration of the Trinity as Divine Love "enworlded." Ultimately, this trinitarian "enworlding" looks to a world "trinified," as the world, the entire cosmos, is drawn into the universe of divine Love. "In the giving of the Word and Spirit into the world the trinitarian selfhood of God is enworlding itself: and from the other standpoint, the world is becoming trinified."[116] Through this kind of interconnection, a technique that is so strong and characteristic a feature of Kelly's theology (together with that of eschatological liberation, the third technique of theological reflection to which Vatican I referred),

Kelly perceives that the Trinity and creation are configured: the Trinity is "enworlded" in the missions of the Word and Spirit and creation is "trinified" through the incarnate Word and the indwelling Spirit.

This transposition of trinitarian meaning on the axis of self-giving love and Being-in-love radically affects our way of defining God. Be-ing yields to Being-in-Love. From the perspective of God as Being-in-Love, Kelly broaches the issue of the traditional affirmations of divine impassibility and immutability, classical notions of the divine transcendence which the modern mind finds unpalatable, even offensive.[117] Kelly is acutely aware of the theological issues at stake here, but he recognizes that the concrete realism of Love demands that its invocation of God in this way lives from an affirmation of God as really and truly invocable, relational, relatable, and related in a way that the traditional explication of the divine attributes does not convey. Kelly's exploration would lead us to understand that God does indeed suffer, precisely because God is Love (but not that God suffers our evils in the way that we do). To say that divine Love is compassionate is nothing less than a statement of total self-involvement in creation. As Kelly pithily explains, "God is not transcendentally removed from our existence, but transcendentally involved with it."[118] Kelly also recognizes that "[a]ny separation of the immanent Trinity from the economy of God's self-giving fails to appreciate the real being of God as Love."[119] The distinction is rendered superfluous in a trinitarian theology that is firmly and confidently grounded in its own experiential base. Here is another of the benefits of phenomenologically based understanding of the mystery.

This transposition of trinitarian meaning in terms of Being-in-love likewise radically affects our way of defining ourselves and the agenda for human living. Kelly expounds on the relevance it has and on the real difference it makes to the deeper registers of the individual and collective psyches. We see that, in Kelly's hands, the psychological analogy continues to be genuinely fruitful and productive, just as the divine Word keeps coming to birth and the Holy Spirit proceeds in ever new levels of affectivity in the world. In the psychological character of "the journey inward," the analogy has therapeutic significance. In the outer reaches of the political and social "journey outward," it introduces a new sense of belonging and engagement in our human history.[120] Finally, Kelly explores how the mystery of the Trinity can be understood as the form, inspiration, and horizon of humanity's religious development and thus can very effectively serve as a foundation for genuine interfaith dialogue.[121]

We see that, in comparison with our other authors, Kelly approaches the mystery of the Trinity in a more traditionally systematic way, transposing the elements of classical trinitarian theology into the phenomenality of Love and resituating the mystery in a framework of Being-in-Love. Basing this transposition on Lonergan's analysis of intentionality wherein the peak state of consciousness is self-transcending being-in-love, the result is a revised ontology in which being is understood, not in terms of substance categories, but in terms of love and the relationality of love. In such a framework, the concept of essence is not external to the category of relation, however.[122] In fact, Kelly argues that, in contrast to the traditional more substance-fashioned concept of the divine essence, such an ontology shows that we can think of the divine essence precisely as epitomized in the personal relations among Father, Son, and Holy Spirit. The fundamental point is that when the root analogy is personal and the foundational reality relational, a very different interpretation and understanding of the divine being emerges, as we have seen.

Such a trinitarian ontology sublates rather than negates its classical antecedent. Kelly insists that being-in-love does not mean the exclusion of be-ing.[123] Nor does it mean the exclusion of being-as-knowing. After all, to love and to know are not mutually exclusive. Both constitute the dynamics of self-transcending subjectivity. Kelly implies that it is the *balance* of knowing and loving that needs attention in trinitarian theology and, from this perspective, his transposition functions to redress an imbalance in the traditional method of explication whereby knowing is accorded priority, resulting in an intellectual distortion in trinitarian theology to which theologians such as von Balthasar rightly object.

Kelly contends that the transposition of scholastic categories into phenomenologically based experience better satisfies the religious imagination and better meets the demands of contemporary theological thinking, affording a fuller appreciation of the trinitarian mystery which is implicated in faith's experience. In terms of the existential imagination, the analogy of love expresses the profoundly personal character of the Trinity. It allows the systematic starting point to be personal, namely the Father as infinite original self-giving Love, expressing himself in the Word and communicating himself in the Spirit. The Thomistically dominant notion of God as undifferentiated Be-ing is in this way more clearly contextualized and personalized in the concrete mystery of Love.

Tony Kelly's retrieval of classical trinitarian theology is the fruit of mature and imaginative reflection on contemporary consciousness and its exigences. His critical reappropriation of the psychological analogy is securely grounded in a thorough knowledge of the tradition of Christian thought and doctrine and, at the same time, it is deeply informed by the wide expanses of contemporary thought. What is especially noteworthy is that the psychological analogy, when transposed in this kind of way, once again *serves* an understanding of the triune God who is revealed in Jesus Christ as love. In this way, Kelly offers a very salutary reminder to trinitarian theology that the classical psychological analogy cannot responsibly be summarily dismissed and that, when appropriately transposed, it may continue to enjoy considerable explicative power, as is evident in the variety of applications Kelly himself attempts.[124]

7
Conclusion

Our explorations of five contemporary developments in trinitarian theology manifestly attest to the continuing fascination of the
Trinity for contemporary theologians. The theology of each age
must respond to new issues and pastoral concerns. New sensibili-
ties, concerns, and modes of consciousness must be met. Faithfulness to the doctrines of our faith and to the Christian realism which
grounds those doctrine demands a rearticulation of that realism in
ways that effectively realize it anew in different contexts. Far from
betraying or forsaking the long and dearly held truths of our Christian tradition, such endeavors seek to mediate the meaning of the
articles of faith ever more effectively to us, expressing the truths we
profess in newly compelling and indeed transforming ways for the
here-and-now of our lives and our faith.

Our authors' concerns, in fact, reflect the change of culture
and emergence of new forms of consciousness that have occurred,
as well as the breakdown of what we can describe, in fairly technical terms, as the theoretic form of mediation of meaning that pre-
vailed in the scholastic period. The traditional explication is
rendered obsolete for we no longer inhabit Aquinas's cultural and
conceptual universe. The classical metaphysically fashioned psychological analogy, which has for so long dominated considerations of the immanent Trinity, is no longer adequate or appropriate
to the modern mind in its search for understanding of the faith we

confess. In a more empirically organized culture, the contemporary theological imagination rightly turns its attention to attempt to express the mystery in more experientially and existentially meaningful ways. Reconceived in these fresh ways that we have examined, ways that are attuned to modern consciousness and its exigences, a theology of the Trinity emerges as a vital and resonant theological centerpiece in which the other theological truths find their meaning and point of connection. So should it be.

A Thematic Overview

Let us now take an overall perspective on the areas of development which we have explored. First, we note that all of our authors stand firmly in the Catholic theological tradition, but all recognize a certain inadequacy in the traditional Augustinian-Thomistic Latin approach to trinitarian theology. Each seeks to refashion trinitarian theology to meet a new range of questions. Different contexts, audiences, and pastoral and theological concerns profoundly affect the trinitarian theologies that emerge. Boff's liberation trinitarian theology in effect addresses the concerns of the nonperson—the one who is dehumanized, oppressed by poverty, marginalized from political participation by patriarchal social structures, that all too easily find their justification in monarchical monotheism. Johnson's feminist trinitarian theology exposes and seeks to redress the denial of the full humanity of women and, indeed, the diminishment of the humanity of *all* men and women that is the result of an unbalanced and uncritical use of masculinist conceptions of God. Edwards' ecological trinitarian theology recognizes that the fullness of our humanity is integrally related to an appreciation of the dignity and sacredness of the whole cosmos and of all creation, for everywhere and everything in creation is redolent of its trinitarian creator. In contrast to classical trinitarian theology and the psychological analogy which is expressed in terms of the individual human consciousness, these three authors opt, although in very different ways, for a distinctly social model of the Trinity. They look for and find in the mystery of the Trinity the inspiration, indeed the demand, for a fuller realization of genuinely human lives that are to be concretely realized in practical, socio-political, and ethical terms, in society, in the church, and in our responsibility to care for the universe and the diversity of life within it.

These authors thus work to great leverage the powerful practical ramifications of a social model of the Trinity for human society, for being human in the human community and in the community that is the cosmos itself. In Boff, Johnson, and Edwards, we find a particularly strong emphasis on the principles of equality, mutuality, reciprocity, and inclusion, and a model of the Trinity that orients us into the world of relationship and communion. In a more explicitly pastoral and spiritual vein, but without much explicit reference to the authors we have been treating, Mary Timothy Prokes, S.S.N.D., also explores the meaning of mutuality in trinitarian relations in order to perceive anew the human vocation to live as image of this divine mutual love. She provides a series of valuable examples of mutuality within the church: an innercity parish, two vibrant lay communities, and a Benedictine abbey—each in its distinctive manner, earths and incarnates, however imperfectly, the human image of trinitarian love in our own time, in particular places, among specific people.[125]

In these ways, these trinitarian theologies effectively express and, in very real and concrete terms, fully intend a trinitarian orthopraxis. They would persuade us that our faith in the Trinity has ethical consequences, that it makes profoundly practical demands of us. They challenge us to a daily trinitarian examination of conscience. It is almost as if, after two thousand years of attention to matters of trinitarian orthodoxy—the "right teaching" with respect to the Trinity—that now at last we have come to the point of seeking a trinitarian orthopraxis, the "right practice." Not that Johnson's work can be relegated simply to a trinitarian orthopraxis. Her feminist consciousness is acutely aware of the power of the symbol in shaping meaning and self-identity, individually and collectively, and this pushes her further still to deconstruct the traditional trinitarian symbol, constructed in masculinist terms, and to reconstruct it using expressly female imagery.

Both Johnson and Edwards find Wisdom Christology a vital wellspring from which to develop their trinitarian theologies. It is hardly surprising that, in their theologies, the person of the Holy Spirit emerges with particular liveliness and vitality. In fact, Johnson begins her explication of the Trinity with the person of the Holy Spirit, here too exposing an implicit and too often taken for granted hierarchicalism in the tradition. For both Boff and Johnson, the notion of the human person created in the image of God, *imago Dei,* and therefore *imago Trinitatis,* is a critical insight with far reaching ramifications for human social and political behavior and organization.

Kelly, on the other hand, comes to trinitarian theology with highly refined methodological interest and sophistication. As we have seen, our other authors effectively reject the psychological analogy. But Kelly takes us back to the scriptural witness to the divine self-giving in Word and Spirit, reminding us that such divine self-communication surely pertains to the divine consciousness, and to the biblical understanding of the human person as created in the image of God. He takes seriously the analogy of consciousness and recognizes that an analysis of the experience of self and its dynamic of self-transcendence (our openness to truth and value) provides the means for a credible and creditable transposition of the classical analogy into more meaningful experiential terms. In this way, Kelly deftly achieves a critical retrieval of the psychological analogy that grounds the analogy once again in our concrete conscious experience of selfhood in its individual, social, and global dimensions. Kelly demonstrates that the analogy, thus relocated, is well able to serve with considerable fruitfulness faith's experience that God is love.

Be it the more social model for the Trinity or the more interior model of consciousness, analogy technically speaking, we find that both approaches have significant yields for Christian practice and community. In these kinds of ways, the doctrine of the Trinity serves to deconstruct those habits of mind or of heart that inhibit our self-transcendence in self-giving in community. Kelly meets Edwards in a Trinity-grounded ecological theology. The Franciscan approach, succinctly expressed in Bonaventure's notion of exemplarity wherein all creation, as a whole and as individual creatures, bears the imprint of the Trinity, converges with the Augustinian Thomistic understanding of being as participation in the divine life. Both attempt to express the one profound mystery—God dwelling in us and us dwelling in God, which the New Testament attests. Both converge in an understanding of the sacredness of life and a reverence for it in all its diversity. The human person emerges with an even more sacred role and responsibility, sharing with the Creator Trinity in the care and custodianship of all creation.

Von Balthasar is something of a maverick in this field. He is not immediately concerned for the social ramifications of trinitarian theology or for the psychological analogy, no matter how sophisticated a retrieval. Doxology, rather than praxis, is his primary concern, so enraptured is he by the iconic disclosure of the divine in the paschal mystery itself and so mystically captivated by the sheer radiance of it. Von Balthasar thus has interest neither in social models nor in analogies from human consciousness when he comes to an explication of the mystery of the Trinity. Such models and analogies simply pale into insignificance in comparison with the revelation of the mystery of God that is given in the paschal mystery of Jesus. For von Balthasar, something much more vital is at stake in a theology of the Trinity—the very mystery of God and the sheer glory of it. He finds in the Trinity's self-expression in the paschal mystery of Jesus and, in particular, the descent into hell, the signal expression of the otherwise unimaginable glory and utter splendor of the love of God.

In a penetrating response to protest atheism, von Balthasar sees that the descent into hell manifests just how deeply God comes to find us in the depths of our suffering, desolation, and despair. The descent reveals that all creation, even hell—a necessary consequence of genuine freedom—is mysteriously taken up into the very being of God. His theology of Trinity, expressed as it is in affectively charged aesthetic-dramatic categories, resonates with the contemporary affective experience of the self with remarkable power.[126] The theological yield from von Balthasar's extraordinary project is most especially evident in his refashioning of an understanding of the divine perfections, particularly the notions of immutability and impassibility (and here Kelly, from a more traditionally systematic perspective, and von Balthasar meet). At the very least, von Balthasar's trinitarian explorations radically call into question the hegemony which the psychological analogy has enjoyed in trinitarian theology for almost two millennia. More than this, however, they call for a closer mediation between God's self-revelation and the faith of the church.

What clearly emerges from these Trinitarian reconstructions, some more radical and more critical than others, is the profoundly relational character of the mystery. Despite all their differences and distinctiveness, each of these theologies effectively reworks traditional trinitarian categories into more dynamic, personalist, and relational terms. The traditional theological categories of nature, essence, substance, while not rejected, are transformed when situated in the context of an ontology of love. While processions, relations, persons, and missions continue to serve as key terms in the elucidation of the trinitarian mystery, these traditional categories of trinitarian theology are substantially refashioned. The understanding of the divine persons and their relations is rendered in a more dynamic fashion. The relations are not the rather immobilist relations of origin or subsistent relations in the immanent Trinity, as traditionally expounded: they are the relations of interpersonal love. The processions are not elucidated in terms of a faculty analysis but rather in terms of the vital relationality of love. While personhood is explicated in explicitly relational terms, mission is recast in more personal and historical terms. The intensely relational notion of perichoresis serves as a vital linchpin, effectively replacing more substantialist notions of the divine unity. In other words, the traditional metaphysically fashioned categories yield to a more concrete, psychologically fashioned mode of expression. The traditional substance categories consequently recede in importance and yield to more affectively charged personalist categories of love and the relationality which is constitutive of love. The category of relationality becomes central.

A much more nuanced understanding of the divine attributes also emerges—particularly in regard to the traditional notions of divine impassibility and immutability. The divine perfections are the perfections of love. Even the question of relationship between the immanent and economic Trinity recedes in importance in these trinitarian theologies, grounded more obviously as they are in faith's experience of divine love. The classical notion of appropriation similarly recedes in importance because the unique and proper character of each of the divine persons is appreciated in their common work of love.

Grounding it all is a vital sense of the Love that God is. As Simone Weil expressed it: God is love the way an emerald is green. The Thomistic synthesis expressed the divine mystery in terms of the sheer "to be" of God *(Ipsum Esse),* communicating itself to creation. Transposing this emphasis into the divine self-gift as love, God is more deeply appreciated and adored as sheer "being-in-love," to use Kelly's expression. All of the trinitarian theologies we have considered point to this great mystery. They insist on grounding an understanding of the Trinity in terms of God as love and the relationality and mutuality of love.

A Methodological Overview

Methodologically, we can understand the plurality of these developments in trinitarian theology in terms of Bernard Lonergan's intentionality analysis. The plurality demonstrates the occurrence of an ever fuller subjectivity of religious and specifically Christian experience being integrated into the theological enterprise. What we have in effect is different differentiations of consciousness coming to the theological question of the Trinity: a politically attuned differentiation of consciousness, sharply honed in the desperate situation of poverty and oppression in Latin America (Boff); the feminist consciousness, acutely aware of the pervasive presence and dehumanizing effect of sexism in the tradition (Johnson); the ecological consciousness that responds to and inspires a cosmic sense of the mystery of the Trinity (Edwards); the aesthetic-dramatic consciousness, so captivated and enraptured by the sheer drama of the inner-trinitarian event, with its gaze focused on Jesus as the form of God's self-revelation (von Balthasar); and the systematic-interiorly differentiated consciousness, appropriating the modern data of consciousness into trinitarian theology (Kelly).

Lonergan's analysis of differentiations of consciousness is, in this way, applicable to the description and assessment of the differences that our exploration of recent developments in trinitarian theology presents to us. This is helpful, not only in methodologically situating and making sense of very different theologies in relation to each other, but in enhancing an understanding of their respective contributions and, moreover, thereby furthering the possibility of theological dialogue. It is not that theology is like a smorgasbord for the believer to pick and choose at will and whim. The point is that each of the trinitarian theologies we have explored is, in effect, attuned to and mediates meaning to differentiations of consciousness in the human community. The task is not only legitimate but imperative for us, be it is as pastors, preachers, or teachers, as we seek to express the mysteries of Christian faith in ways that are meaningful to those with whom we are communicating.

In Lonergan's terms, we can describe this whole shift in theological method and practice as a shift into the third stage of meaning, where meaning is not expressed in theoretical categories (as in the Thomistic synthesis) but in terms of consciousness which is differentiated in manifold diversity.[127] Theology in this third stage of meaning will not be the systematic, rigorous, and logically exacting synthesis that it was in the second stage, where the exigence of theory prevails. It is, in contrast, characterized by pluralism, such as we see in our five authors here—a pluralism that is the fruit of variously differentiated converted consciousnesses, each seeking to understand and to communicate the meaning of the Christian mysteries. This is what we mean when we describe the development which we have observed in our survey as evidence of the occurrence of an ever fuller subjectivity being integrated into the theological enterprise. Far from sacrificing any objectivity, however, this development promises ever closer approximations to the objective truth of the mysteries we seek to express. As Lonergan recognized, objective truth is the fruit of genuine subjectivity: "...objectivity is simply the consequence of authentic subjectivity, of genuine attention, genuine intelligence, genuine reasonableness, genuine responsibility."[128]

So we come to the conclusion of our exploration of newly emerging directions in trinitarian theology. We have explored various efforts to mediate the meaning of our belief in the Trinity. Each aims to give explicitly trinitarian shape and meaning to our faith, hope, and love. Each points to the mystery of the Trinity as our home, in which we live and move and have our being. Each moves the mystery of the Trinity from the background to the foreground of our thinking, our believing, our praying, our living, our loving, our dying, and our rising. All to the greater glory of our three-personed God.

Notes

1. For surveys of classical trinitarian theology, see especially Bertrand de Margerie, *The Christian Trinity in History,* Studies in Historical Theology, vol. I, trans. Edmund J. Fortman (Petersham, MA: St. Bede's Publications, 1982); Edmund J. Fortman, *The Triune God: A Historical Study of the Doctrine of the Trinity* (London: Hutchinson, 1972); William J. Hill, *The Three-Personed God: The Trinity as a Mystery of Salvation* (Washington, DC: Catholic University of America Press, 1982); Thomas Marsh, *The Triune God: A Biblical, Historical and Theological Study* (Maynooth Bicentenary Series. Blackrock, Co. Dublin: Columba Press, 1994).

2. As well as the sources cited above, see Edmund Hill, *The Mystery of the Trinity,* Introducing Catholic Theology Series (London: Geoffrey Chapman, 1985).

3. In his search for trinitarian analogies, Augustine considers, for example, the faculties of memory, knowledge and love; memory, knowledge and love of self; and the activity of remembering God, understanding God, and willing or loving God. Augustine also considers the triad of the loving subject, the object loved, and the relation of love which unites them, later taken up by the twelfth century monastic theologian, Richard of Saint Victor. See *The Trinity, The Works of Saint Augustine:* A Translation for the 21st Century Series, with an Introduction, translation and notes by Edmund Hill (Brooklyn, NY: New City Press, 1991).

4. For discussions of Aquinas's work, see David B. Burrell,

Aquinas: God and Action (Notre Dame, IN: University of Notre Dame Press, 1979); Brian Davies, *The Thought of Thomas Aquinas* (Oxford: Clarendon Press, 1992); Douglas C. Hall, *The Trinity: An Analysis of St. Thomas Aquinas' Expositio of the De Trinitate of Boethius* (Leiden: E. J. Brill, 1992); W. J. Hankey, *God in Himself: Aquinas' Doctrine of God as Expounded in the Summa Theologiae* (Oxford: Oxford University Press, 1987); Bernard Lonergan, *Verbum: Word and Idea in Aquinas* (London: Darton, Longman & Todd, 1967); Donald Juvenal Merriell, *To the Image of the Trinity: A Study in the Development of Aquinas' Teaching* (Toronto: Pontifical Institute of Mediaeval Studies, 1990).

5. So Thomas himself describes his effort in the Prologue to the *Summa Theologiae*.

6. Karl Rahner, *Foundations of Christian Faith: An Introduction to the Idea of Christianity,* trans. William V. Dych (New York: Crossroad, 1987), 135.

7. Karl Rahner, *The Trinity,* trans. Joseph Donceel (London: Burns and Oates, 1970), 21–4.

8. For a classic text on the Trinity and interfaith dialogue, see Raimundo Panikkar, *The Trinity and the Religious Experience of Man* (London: DLT, 1973).

9. For an excellent introduction to liberation theology, see Ignacio Ellacuria and Jon Sobrino, eds., *Mysterium Liberationis: Fundamental Concepts of Liberation Theology* (Maryknoll, NY: Orbis, 1993).

10. Gustavo Gutiérrez, *A Theology of Liberation,* trans. Sister Caridad Inda and John Eagleson (Maryknoll, NY: Orbis, 1973; revised edition, 1998).

11. For a classic in the area of liberation Christology, see Jon Sobrino, *Christology at the Crossroads: A Latin American Approach,* trans. John Drury (Maryknoll, NY: Orbis, 1978); idem, *Jesus in Latin America* (Maryknoll, NY: Orbis, 1987). Also Leonardo Boff, *Jesus Christ Liberator: A Critical Christology for Our Time,* trans. Patrick Hughes (Maryknoll, NY: Orbis, 1978).

12. Leonardo Boff, *Trinity and Society,* Liberation and Theology Series, No. 2, trans. Paul Burns (London: Burns and Oates, 1988), 158.

13. *Ibid.,* 163.

14. *Ibid.,* 399.

15. *Ibid.,* 137.

16. *Ibid.,* 152.

17. *Ibid.,* 148ff.

18. *Ibid.,* 120.

19. *Ibid.,* 11.

20. *Ibid.,* 7.

21. *Ibid.,* 119.

22. *Ibid.,* 151.

23. Boff, "Trinity" in *Mysterium Liberationis: Fundamental Concepts of Liberation Theology* (Maryknoll, NY: Orbis, 1993), 392.

24. *Trinity and Society,* 153.

25. *Ibid.,* 154.

26. *Ibid.,* 22–3.

27. *Ibid.,* 164–177.

28. *Ibid.,* 175.

29. *Ibid.,* 177.

30. *Ibid.,* 170–1

31. *Ibid.,* 178–88.

32. *Ibid.,* 182–5.

33. *Ibid.,* 183.

34. *Ibid.,* 189–218.

35. *Ibid.,* 196–8.

36. *Ibid.,* 198.

37. *Ibid.,* 193.

38. *Ibid.,* 208.

39. For a classic feminist theological text, see Rosemary Radford Ruether, *Sexism and God-Talk: Toward a Feminist Theology* (Boston: Beacon Press, 1983).

40. Mary Daly, *Beyond God the Father: Toward a Philosophy of Women's Liberation* (Boston: Beacon Press, 1973), 19.

41. H. Denzinger and A. Sch`enmetzer, eds., *Enchiridion Symbolorum: Definitionum et Declarationum de Rebus Fidei et Morum*, 32d edition (Freiburg: Herder, 1963), 806. This text hereafter referred to as DS.

42. Elizabeth Johnson, *She Who Is: the Mystery of God in Feminist Theological Discourse* (New York: Crossroad, 1992), 33–34. Hereafter cited as She Who Is.

43. *She Who Is*, 5.

44. Bernard Lonergan, *Insight*, 191–203, 222–5.

45. *She Who Is*, 26

46. *Ibid.*, 193.

47. *Ibid.*, 196.

48. Johnson, "The Incomprehensibility of God and the Image of God Male and Female." *Theological Studies* 45 (1984): 463.

49. *She Who Is*, 124–49.

50. *Ibid.*, 150–69.

51. *Ibid.*, 167.

52. *Ibid.*, 168.

53. *Ibid.*, 170–87.

54. *Ibid.*, 185.

55. *Ibid.*, 217ff.

56. *Summa Theologiae*, Ia, 13, 11.

57. *Ibid.*, 243.

58. Simone Weil, *Waiting for God* (London: Routledge and Kegan Paul, 1950), 100.

59. Denis Edwards, Jesus, *The Wisdom of God: An Ecological Theology* (Homebush, N.S.W.: St Paul's, 1995). Hereafter referred to as *Jesus, The Wisdom of God.*

60. *Jesus, The Wisdom of God,* 13.

61. *Ibid.*, 15.

62. *Ibid.*, 19.

63. Dante, in *Divine Comedy,* speaks of "the Love that moves the sun and the other stars."

64. Quoted by Edwards in *Jesus the Wisdom of God,* 97, from Richard of St. Victor's De Trinitate, III.19 (Translation from Grover Zinn, *Richard of St. Victor,* 379).

65. Zachary Hayes, *Works of Saint Bonaventure: III Saint Bonaventure's Disputed Questions on the Mystery of the Trinity, Introduction and Translation* (The Franciscan University, New York, 1979), 27. Hayes' *Introduction* is an excellent resource for those wishing to study Bonaventure's trinitarian theology in more detail.

66. See Hayes' *Introduction,* 46f, for an explanation of the critical role which exemplarity plays in Bonaventure's theology.

67. *Jesus, The Wisdom of God,* 111f.

68. *Ibid.,* 115. See also Edwards' article "The Discovery of Chaos and the Retrieval of the Trinity" in *Chaos and Complexity: Scientific Perspectives on Divine Action,* eds. R. J. Russell, N. Murphy and A. R. Peacocke (Vatican City State: Vatican Observatory Publications, 1995. Berkeley, CA: The Center for Theology, 1995) 157–75.

69. *Jesus, The Wisdom of God,* 122.

70. *Ibid.,* 127–8.

71. *Ibid.,* 129–30.

72. *Ibid.,* 117.

73. *Ibid.,* 154–5.

74. *Ibid.,* 143.

75. Hans Urs von Balthasar, *Love Alone: The Way of Revelation,* ed. Alexander Dru (London: Burns & Oates, 1968), 7–8.

76. *Ibid.,* 71.

77. *Mysterium Paschale: The Mystery of Easter.* Trans. with an Introduction by Aidan Nichols (Edinburgh: T&T Clark, 1990), 29. Hereafter referred to as *Mysterium Paschale.*

78. *Prayer,* trans. Graham Harrison (San Francisco: Ignatius Press, 1986), 184.

79. *Mysterium Paschale*, viii.

80. *Theodramatik*, vol. III, *Die Handlung* (Einsiedeln: Johannes Verlag, 1980), 302.

81. *Mysterium Paschale*, viii.

82. *Theo-Drama: Theological Dramatic Theory*, vol I, *Prolegomena*, trans. Graham Harrison (San Francisco: Ignatius Press, 1988), 20.

83. *Theodramatik*, III:304.

84. *Prayer*, 188.

85. *Mysterium Paschale*, 91.

86. Thomas Aquinas, *Summa Theologiae*, 3a. 3, 5.

87. *Theo-Drama*, III:207. See also "On the Concept of Person," *Communio* 13 (1986): 18–26.

88. Of the relationship of his work to that of von Speyr, von Balthasar writes: "Her work and mine are neither psychologically nor philologically to be separated: two halves of a single whole which has as its center a unique foundation." *My Work: In Retrospect* (San Francisco: Communio Books Ignatius Press, 1993), 89, see also 19, 30, 105–7.

89. *The Von Balthasar Reader*, eds. Kehl, Medard, and Werner Löser, trans. Robert J. Daly and Fred Lawrence (Edinburgh: T&T Clark, 1985), 404.

90. *The Von Balthasar Reader*, 153.

91. *Ibid.*, 152–3.

92. *Elucidations*, trans. John Riches (London: SPCK, 1975), 53.

93. *The Von Balthasar Reader*, 422.

94. *Elucidations*, 51.

95. *The Glory of the Lord VII*, 233.

96. *Mysterium Paschale*, 191.

97. *Ibid.*, 204.

98. *Ibid.*, 211.

99. *Theodramatik*, III:304.

100. *Life Out of Death: Meditations on the Easter Mystery,* trans. Davis Perkins (Philadelphia: Fortress Press, 1985), 39.

101. *Mysterium Paschale,* vii–ix, 23–41.

102. Vatican II, *Pastoral Constitution on the Church in the Modern World* (Gaudium et Spes), par 5.

103. For discussion of process theology, see William J. Hill, *The Three-Personed God: The Trinity as a Mystery of Salvation,* 201.

104. Kelly, *The Trinity of Love: A Theology of the Christian God,* New Theology Series No. 4 (Wilmington, Delaware: Michael Glazier, 1989), hereafter referred to as *Trinity of Love.* See also Kelly's *Expanding Theology: Faith in a World of Connections* (Newtown, N.S.W.: E. J. Dwyer, 1993); and idem "The 'Horrible Wrappers' of Aquinas' God," Pacifica 9 (1996): 185–203.

105. *Constitution on Divine Revelation* (Dei Filius) DS 3016.

106. *Trinity of Love,* 191.

107. See especially *Trinity of Love* 139–73.

108. William Norris Clarke stands firmly in the Thomistic tradition and, alert to modern phenomenology, offers a metaphysical foundation which is able to contribute to this retrieval of Thomist trinitarian theology. See especially Clarke, *Person and Being,* The Aquinas Lecture, 1993 (Milwaukee: Marquette University Press, 1993).

109. Bernard J. F. Lonergan, *De Deo Trino I. Pars Dogmatica and II. Pars Systematica* (Rome: Pontificia Universitas Gregoriana, 1964).

110. See, especially, Lonergan, *Method in Theology; Collection,* Collected Works of Bernard Lonergan. Vol. 4. 2d rev. and aug. ed., ed. Frederick E. Crowe and Robert M. Doran. (Toronto: University of Toronto Press for Lonergan Research Institute of Regis College, 1988); *A Second Collection: Papers by Bernard J.F. Lonergan, S.J.,* eds. William F.J. Ryan and Bernard J. Tyrrell

(London: Darton, Longman and Todd, 1974); *A Third Collection: Papers by Bernard J.F. Lonergan, S.J.*, ed. Frederick E. Crowe (New York: Paulist Press, 1985).

111. *Method in Theology,* 120.

112. *Ibid.,* 105.

113. *Trinity of Love,* 189–95.

114. *Ibid.,* 184–89.

115. *Ibid.,* 111.

116. *Ibid.,* 97.

117. *Ibid.,* 195–202.

118. *Ibid.,* 200.

119. *Ibid.,* 179.

120. *Ibid.,* 203–27.

121. *Ibid.,* 228–48.

122. William Norris Clarke, S.J., also insists that theology must not deny person as substance, for person is not simply relation. Without the dimension of substance, the notion of person loses its metaphysical grounding. Both substance and relation are primordial modes of reality. See especially Clarke, *Person and Being.*

123. See Kelly's article, "The 'Horrible Wrappers' of Aquinas' God," *Pacifica* 9 (1996): 185–203.

124. See Kelly, *An Expanding Theology: Faith in a World of Connections.*

125. Mary Timothy Prokes, *Mutuality: The Human Image of Trinitarian Love* (Mahwah, NJ: Paulist Press, 1993).

126. For discussions of von Balthasar's theology and its extraordinarily evocative power, see Robert Doran's discussions. Doran suggests that the notion of psychic conversion should take its place alongside Lonergan's foundational conversions. Doran thus proposes a distinctly psychological contribution to Lonergan's methodological foundations and offers an even more refined terminology and methodology that is applicable to the deeper psychic reaches of theological subjectivity. Such a notion

does seem to apply to von Balthasar's theology, which seems to lie more clearly in the realm of affect, feeling and symbol than in the realm of intentionality as such; in other words, in the realm of the "psychic" rather than that of the "spiritual," as Doran expresses it. Doran thus offers the possibility of a critical grounding for von Balthasar's theological aesthetics. See Robert M. Doran, *Psychic Conversion and Theological Foundations: Towards a Reorientation of the Human Sciences* (Atlanta, GA: Scholars Press, 1981); idem *Theology and the Dialectics of History* (Toronto: University of Toronto Press, 1990). See also the discussion of Doran in relation to von Balthasar's work in my *The Trinity and the Paschal Mystery* (Collegeville, MN: Liturgical Press, 1997).

127. Lonergan, *Method in Theology,* 85–99.

128. *Ibid.,* 265.

Selected Bibliography and Recommended Reading

Overviews of Trinitarian Theology

de Margerie, Bertrand. *The Christian Trinity in History.* Studies in Historical Theology. Vol. I. Translated by Edmund J. Fortman. Petersham, MA: St. Bede's Publications, 1982.

Fortman, Edmund J. *The Triune God: A Historical Study of the Doctrine of the Trinity.* London: Hutchinson, 1972.

Hill, William J. *The Three-Personed God: The Trinity as a Mystery of Salvation.* Washington, DC: Catholic University of America Press, 1982.

Marsh, Thomas. *The Triune God: A Biblical, Historical and Theological Study.* Maynooth Bicentenary Series. Blackrock, Co Dublin: Columba Press, 1994.

Torrance, T. F. *The Trinitarian Faith.* Edinburgh: T&T Clark, 1988.

———. *The Christian Doctrine of God: One Being Three Persons.* Edinburgh: T&T Clark, 1996.

Latin American Liberation Theology

Boff, Leonardo and Clodovis. *Introducing Liberation Theology.* Maryknoll, NY: Orbis, 1987.

Boff, Leonardo. *Trinity and Society.* Liberation and Theology

Series. No. 2. Translated by Paul Burns. London: Burns and Oates, 1988.

Ellacuria, Ignacio and Sobrino, Jon, Editors. *Mysterium Liberationis: Fundamental Concepts of Liberation Theology*. Maryknoll, NY: Orbis, 1993. 389–404.

Gutiérrez, Gustavo. *A Theology of Liberation.* Translated by Sister Caridad Inda and John Eagleson. Maryknoll, NY: Orbis, 1973; revised edition, 1998.

Feminist Theology

Fiorenza, Elisabeth Schussler. *In Memory of Her: A Feminist Theological Reconstruction of Christian Origins*. New York: Crossroad, 1983.

Johnson, Elizabeth A. *She Who Is: The Mystery of God in Feminist Theological Discourse*. New York: Crossroad, 1992.

————."The Incomprehensibility of God and the Image of God Male and Female." *Theological Studies* 45 (1984): 441–65.

Kimel, Alvin F. Jr., ed. *Speaking the Christian God: The Holy Trinity and the Challenge of Feminism.* Grand Rapids: Eerdmans, 1992.

LaCugna, Catherine Mowry. *God for Us: The Trinity and Christian Life*. New York: HarperCollins, 1991.

Ruether, Rosemary Radford. *Sexism and God-Talk: Towards a Feminist Theology*. Boston: Beacon Press, 1983.

Trinity and Ecology

Edwards, Denis. *Jesus, the Wisdom of God: An Ecological Theology*. Homebush, N.S.W.: St Paul's, 1995.

Kelly, Tony. *An Expanding Theology: Faith in a World of Connections*. Newtown, N.S.W.: E. J. Dwyer, 1993.

McFague, Sallie. *The Body of God: An Ecological Theology*. Minneapolis: Fortress Press, 1993.

Trinity and Paschal Mystery

Hunt, Anne. *The Trinity and the Paschal Mystery*. Collegeville, MN: Liturgical Press, 1997.

Kehl, Medard, and Werner Löser, eds. *The Von Balthasar Reader*. Translated by Robert J. Daly and Fred Lawrence. Edinburgh: T&T Clark, 1985.

O'Hanlon, Gerard F. *The Immutability of God in the Theology of Hans Urs von Balthasar*. Cambridge: Cambridge University Press, 1990.

Saward, John *The Mysteries of March: Hans Urs von Balthasar on Incarnation and Easter*. London: Collins, 1990.

von Balthasar, Hans Urs. *Love Alone: The Way of Revelation: A Theological Perspective*. Edited by Alexander Dru. London: Burns & Oates, 1968.

―――. *The Glory of the Lord: A Theological Aesthetics*. Vol. I, *Seeing the Form*. Edited by Joseph Fessio, S.J. and John Riches. Translated by Erasmo Leiva-Merikakis. San Francisco: Ignatius Press, 1982.

―――. *Prayer*. Translated by Graham Harrison. San Francisco: Ignatius Press, 1986.

―――. *The Glory of the Lord: A Theological Aesthetics*. Vol. VII, *Theology: The New Covenant*. Edited by John Riches. Translated by Brian McNeil. San Francisco: Ignatius Press, 1989.

―――. *Mysterium Paschale: The Mystery of Easter*. Translated with an Introduction by Aidan Nichols. Edinburgh: T&T Clark, 1990.

―――. *Credo: Meditations on the Apostles' Creed*. Translated by David Kipp. New York: Crossroad, 1990.

Trinity and Love

Clarke, W. Norris. "Person, Being and St. Thomas." *Communio* 19 (1992): 601–18.

————. *Person and Being.* The Aquinas Lecture, 1993. Milwaukee: Marquette University Press, 1993.

Kelly, Anthony. *The Trinity of Love: A Theology of the Christian God.* New Theology Series. No. 4. Wilmington, Delaware: Michael Glazier, 1989.

————. (Kelly, Tony) *An Expanding Theology: Faith in a World of Connections.* Newtown, N.S.W.: E. J. Dwyer, 1993.

————. "The 'Horrible Wrappers' of Aquinas' God" *Pacifica* 9 (1996): 185–203.

Other Helpful References

Fatula, Mary Anne. *The Triune God of Christian Faith.* Collegeville, MN: Liturgical Press, 1990.

Hill, Edmund. *The Mystery of the Trinity.* Introducing Catholic Theology Series. London: Geoffrey Chapman, 1985.

Mascall, E. L. *The Triune God: An Ecumenical Study.* Oxford: Blackwell, 1986.

O'Donnell, John J. *The Mystery of the Triune God.* Heythrop Monograph Series. No. 6. London: Sheed & Ward, 1988.

————. *Hans Urs von Balthasar.* Outstanding Christian Thinkers Series. London: Geoffrey Chapman, 1992.

Panikkar, Raimundo. *The Trinity and the Religious Experience of Man.* London: Dartman, Longman & Todd, 1973.

Prokes, Mary Timothy. *Mutuality: The Human Image of Trinitarian Love.* Mahwah, NJ: Paulist Press, 1993.

Rahner, Karl. *The Trinity.* Translated by Joseph Donceel. London: Burns and Oates, 1970.

————. *Foundations of Christian Faith: An Introduction to the Idea of Christianity.* Translated by William V. Dych. New York: Crossroad, 1987.

Rusch, William G. Transl./Ed. *The Trinitarian Controversy.* Sources of Early Christian Thought Series. Philadelphia: Fortress Press, 1980.

Weinandy, Thomas G. *The Father's Spirit of Sonship: Reconceiving the Trinity*. Edinburgh: T&T Clark, 1995.

Zizioulas, John D. *Being as Communion: Studies in Personhood and the Church*. With a Foreword by John Meyendorff. Crestwood, NY: St. Vladimir's Seminary Press, 1985.

———. "The Church as Communion." *St. Vladimir's Theological Quarterly* 38 (1994) 3–16.

Other Books in This Series

What are they saying about the Prophets?
by David P. Reid, SS. CC.
What are they saying about Moral Norms?
by Richard M. Gula, S.S.
What are they saying about Sexual Morality?
by James P. Hanigan
What are they saying about Dogma?
by William E. Reiser, S.J.
What are they saying about Peace and War?
by Thomas A. Shannon
What are they saying about Papal Primacy?
by J. Michael Miller, C.S.B.
What are they saying about Matthew's Sermon on the Mount?
by Donald Senior, C.P.
What are they saying about Biblical Archaeology?
by Leslie J. Hoppe. O.F.M.
What are they saying about Theological Method?
by J.J. Mueller, S.J.
What are they saying about Virtue?
by Anthony J. Tambasco
What are they saying about Genetic Engineering?
by Thomas A. Shannon
What are they saying about Salvation?
by Rev. Denis Edwards
What are they saying about Mark?
by Frank J. Matera
What are they saying about Luke?
by Mark Allan Powell
What are they saying about John?
by Gerard S. Sloyan
What are they saying about Acts?
by Mark Allan Powell
What are they saying about the Ministerial Priesthood?
by Rev. Daniel Donovan

Other Books in This Series

What are they saying about the Social Setting of the New
    Testament?
    by Carolyn Osiek
What are they saying about Scripture and Ethics?
(Revised and Expanded Ed.)
    by William C. Spohn
What are they saying about Unbelief?
    by Michael Paul Gallagher, S.J.
What are they saying about Masculine Spirituality?
    by David James
What are they saying about Environmental Ethics?
    by Pamela Smith
What are they saying about the Formation of Pauline Churches?
    by Richard S. Ascough